FIXED

2

More Answers to Ireland's Frequently Asked Questions

Compiled from Fix It Friday
The Ray D'Arcy Show

MENTOR
BOOKS

First Published in 2004 by

MENTOR BOOKS
43 Furze Road,
Sandyford Industrial Estate,
Dublin 18,
Republic of Ireland.

Tel: + 353 1 295 2112 / 3   Fax: + 353 1 295 2114
e-mail: admin@mentorbooks.ie
www.mentorbooks.ie

ISBN 1-84210-284-2

A catalogue record for this book
is available from the British Library

Text Inputting: Annie McCarthy
Design & Layout: Nicola Sedgwick
Cover Design: Cawley Nea

Printed in Ireland by ColourBooks Ltd.
1 3 5 7 9 10 8 6 4 2

Foreword

Well, I suppose it was inevitable – *Fixed 2*, the sequel. It's the product of idle minds, idle fingers and idle Friday mornings listening to the radio and asking more of those niggly questions.

I don't mean to trivialise the questions herein by referring to them as 'niggly'. They are of course also intelligent, wide-ranging and erudite, as you would expect from our listeners.

There are also the silly ones as well, which we also enjoy, like this one: 'Well Ray, what would you have called the show if it wasn't on a Friday?' Quick as you could say, 'You've too much time oon your hands', our creative and inventive listeners were on the case with more alliterations: Mend it Monday, Tackle It Tuesday, Work It Out Wednesday, Think Tank Thursday and Sort It Out Saturday.

Another question which went to the core of the concept of Fix It Friday was from Chris in Kimmage: 'Why,' he asked, 'do people send questions to you instead of looking the answer up on Google. Are they just too feckin' lazy?' The answer of course is, 'Yes, they are too feckin' lazy'. For this laziness we are eternally thankful, as you should be. After all, their combined curiosity and lack of industry has produced two volumes of essential trivia. (Is that an oxymoron?)

As always we have done our damnedest to deliver definitive answers. However, we may have failed on occasion. That's our nice way of issuing a disclaimer about all the information contained herein.

Thanks to our 'Mountain of Knowledge' Martin Maguire, to Miss FixIt Jenny Kelly, to Mairéad 'I'm Pretty' Farrell, to Will 'New Boy' Hanafin, to Annie, Claire, Nicola and all at Mentor Books. Also thanks to Danny and Willie, the Boss-men, and to Brian and Aidan in the Music Department.

Special thanks to all those experts who shared their knowledge with us and the biggest of big thank yous to all the constantly inquisitive listeners of *The Ray D'Arcy Show* – we couldn't do it without you.

Enough verbiage from me. Enjoy the book and remember – if you don't ask questions you won't get any answers!

Ray D'Arcy

Contents

THE BODY

Female breasts are like Scalectrix –
they're intended for the kids but dads
get more fun out of them.

Why do you always want to pee thirty
seconds after getting in the bath?

Q —

Why do some people have birthmarks?

A —

In fact, almost everyone has some type of birthmark. About one in three infants has a noticeable birthmark and twice as many girls as boys have one. They are most often located on the head or neck but can be found anywhere on the body. Birthmarks are called by a number of popular names – 'strawberry mark,' 'port–wine stain', 'stork bite'. The correct term is haemangioma. Birthmarks are the result of an abnormal distribution of blood vessels during prenatal development; they can be flat or raised. There are many old wives' tales as to the cause of birthmarks but there is no evidence that stressful or traumatic experiences during pregnancy can result in them. Haemangiomas rarely require medical treatment unless they bleed. However, sometimes they are removed for cosmetic reasons. Removal can be by a number of methods including laser treatment, cryosurgery (destruction of tissue by extreme cold), radiotherapy or plastic surgery.

Q —

Who invented false teeth?

A —

Believe it or not the earliest known false teeth date from around 700BC. They were carved from bone or ivory by the Etruscans, who occupied the area which is modern-day Tuscany in Italy.

According to urban legend President George Washington had wooden false teeth. This was not the case. In fact wooden teeth are an impossibility. The corrosive effects of saliva would have turned them into a mushy pulp before long. The first president's teeth came from a variety of sources, including teeth extracted from human and animal corpses.

Q —

If I didn't shave my legs would I eventually trip over my own leg hair?

A —

Probably not. Scalp hair, and facial hair in males, grows continuously. Body hair, on the other hand, displays regular periods of growth and dormancy. During the growth portion of the cycle, body hair follicles are long and bulbous, and the hair grows outward at about a third of a millimetre per day. After a few weeks, growth stops and the hair is as long as it is going to get. The follicle shrinks and the root of the hair stiffens. Following a period of dormancy, another growth cycle starts, and eventually a new hair pushes the old one out of the follicle from beneath. This process doesn't occur simultaneously all over the body or you'd be moulting like a Great Dane! When you shave your legs you are mowing some long, mature hairs as well as some shorter, still-growing ones. And you'll miss some tiny new hairs, which haven't yet protruded above the skin surface, hence the stubble you feel a day or two later.

Why does head hair grow to great length and body hair doesn't? We don't know for sure but some anthropologists believe the functional significance of long head hair is almost certainly adornment, providing for the 'sexual selection' that Darwin argued was a potent factor in the evolutionary process. And, let's face it, long hair usually looks better on heads than legs!

Q —

What, truly, is the average length of a human penis?

A —

Didn't anybody ever tell you that size doesn't matter? But if you really have to know . . . the average length of a flaccid member is approximately 3.5 inches (9 cms); when erect this increases to approximately 5.1 inches (13 cms). (Yes, of course you thought it was more!) Interestingly, there are a number of everyday scents that will help you get from 3.5 to 5.1 by increasing blood flow to the penis. These include lavender, liquorice, chocolate and Homer Simpson's favourite – doughnuts!

Q —

Is there a scientific reason why women open their mouths when applying mascara and eyeliner?

A —

Well, according to our cosmetics sources, you are advised to open your mouth slightly while applying eye make up because, they say, it relaxes your facial muscles. In particular it relaxes the muscles around the eyes which minimises blinking. There is also a neurophysiological explanation. The areas of the brain which control the movements of the mouth and the hands are close together. Concentrated or intricate movement of the hands (applying mascara) can create electrical activity in the brain which spills over into the area that controls the mouth, thus causing movement of the tongue and/or mouth.

Q —

What causes morning sickness?

A —

Morning sickness is caused by rapid changes in hormone levels during the first weeks of pregnancy. It affects approximately half of all pregnant women. It usually begins to ease after the first trimester (three months). There is no guaranteed cure but eating small, frequent meals, including complex carbohydrates, may help. It can also help if you eat something before getting out of bed in the morning as low blood sugar can also cause nausea. Some women have found a vitamin B complex to be helpful but you should consult your doctor before taking any supplements during pregnancy.

Q —

What's the appendix for?

A —

It used to be believed that the appendix had no function and was an evolutionary relic but it is now thought to play a part in the immune system. It contains a large amount of lymphoid tissue, which protects against local infection. It is also believed that it exposes circulating immune cells to antigens from the bacteria and other organisms living in your gut. This helps your immune system to tell friend from foe and stops it from launching damaging attacks on bacteria that happily co-exist with you. However, you can live quite healthily without an appendix and for this reason it can be a useful 'spare part'; it is often used in reconstructive surgery of the bladder without the risk of rejection that would be triggered by using tissue from another person.

Q —

Ray, while I was shaving this morning I got some shaving cream in my ear. I tried to wipe it out but only succeeded in pushing it further in – a minute later I got this disgusting taste at the back of my throat – why?

A —

Because your ears, nose and throat are connected by the Eustachian tube. Its main function is as a drainage passage from the middle ear; it maintains hearing by opening periodically to regulate air pressure. The lower end of the Eustachian tube opens during swallowing and yawning, allowing air to flow up to the middle ear and equalising air pressure on both sides of the eardrum.

Q —

Where does the word 'phlegm' come from and why do we secrete the stuff?

A —

The word comes to us, via Old French and Latin, from ancient Greek. Phlegm is secreted by the mucous membranes in the respiratory system. Its production is increased by infection, an allergic reaction or by inhaling an irritant, e.g. tobacco smoke. Healthy phlegm, or sputum, is usually white or clear. Yellow phlegm is often a sign of an infection and green/brown phlegm is virtually always an indication of infection.

In mediaeval medicine phlegm was considered one of the four bodily humours (the others were blood, choler or yellow bile, and melancholy or black bile) and was believed to be responsible for apathetic or sluggish behaviour, giving us the modern word 'phlegmatic'.

Q —

Why does my stomach grumble when I'm hungry?

A —

The correct term for the growling in your stomach is borborygmus (plural – borborygmi). It happens when your stomach walls do what they should and squeeze together to mix and digest food. If no food is present digestive juices and gases slosh around and you will hear borborygmi.

Q —

What bone is your ulna?

It is one of two bones in your forearm, the other being the radius. The ulna runs parallel to the radius. Its thicker, upper extremity forms a large part of the elbow joint.

Q —

Any chance you could enlighten me as to what DNA stands for?

A —

DNA stands for deoxyribonucleic acid, which is present in the nucleus of every living cell.

Q —

Why do we itch?

A —

The reasons for itching are not completely understood. It can be a symptom of a skin disease or can be caused by something as simple as excessive cleanliness, which strips the skin of its natural oils. Generalised itching can be a symptom of many medical conditions. It can also be an early warning that your body has come into contact with a noxious substance, as in allergy sufferers. In such cases the body releases histamine from white cells. The histamine binds to receptors on local nerve endings causing an itching sensation. Some people find relief from this type of itching by taking anti-histamine preparations.

Q —

My ma's afraid of cats – what does that make her?

A —

She is an ailurophobe; as were, it is alleged, Julius Caesar and Napoleon Bonaparte – does she also display imperial ambitions?

Q —

What happens if you wake someone who is sleepwalking?

A —

Conventional wisdom is that it is best not to try and wake a sleepwalker. Sleepwalkers are usually difficult to wake and can become frightened and disorientated if you try. If you touch them or upset them in any way they may flail about and perhaps hurt you or themselves. Sleepwalkers are capable of completing fairly elaborate tasks, such as getting dressed or making their way to the kitchen or bathroom, without mishap. Most sleepwalking episodes last between five and fifteen minutes and the walker remembers nothing when they wake up.

Q —

What's the difference between a g-string and a thong?

A —

Not a lot, as there is not a lot to either garment! The g-string, as its name suggests, has only a string of fabric instead of a pack panel. The thong contains a little more fabric and usually forms a 'Y' at the waistband. Each is of course designed to do away with the dreaded 'vpl' – visible panty line!

Q —

What is the name for someone who constantly washes their hands?

A —

Repeated hand washing is just one of many possible manifestations of obsessive-compulsive disorder. OCD is a condition that causes people to have unbidden thoughts (obsessions) and to repeat certain behaviours (compulsions) over and over. Some common obsessions are:
– fear of dirt or germs;
– concern with order, symmetry and exactness;

— disgust with bodily waste or fluids;
— thinking about certain sounds, images, words or numbers all the time.

Some common compulsions are:

— constant cleaning and grooming such as hand washing, showering or brushing teeth over and over;
— checking door locks, drawers and appliances to ensure that they are locked, shut or turned off;
— arranging items in a certain way;
— saving junk mail, newspapers or old containers when they are no longer needed

The causes of OCD are uncertain but some research indicates that it may be a lack of serotonin, an important neurotransmitter, in the brain. Treatment for OCD can include drugs or behavioural therapy.

Q —

What is the medical term for colour-blindness?

A —

There are different degrees of colour-blindness. The more common form, which is a congenital inability to distinguish green from red, is known as daltonism. It is named after a nineteenth-century English chemist (John Dalton) who suffered from this complaint. True colour-blindness, where the world is seen only in shades of black, white and grey, is extremely rare and is known as monochromatism. A person who sees no colours at all is described as achromatopic.

How come if I blow into my dog's face he goes mad, but if I take him in the car he wants to stick his head out of the window?

Now the euro is here, where do all the stray dogs go?

Q —

Are elephants afraid of mice?

A —

Elephants are more likely to encounter mice in zoos and circuses (where the abundance of grain and hay will attract them) than in the wild. Given the large size and relatively poor eyesight of elephants, they probably rarely notice the presence of mice and there is no evidence that they fear them. In fact, the elephant is one of the planet's least fearful animals, which is just as well as they share habitats with lions, rhinos, and tigers. Unfortunately, that same fearlessness can also make them easy prey for poachers.

If there's any truth at all to this legend, it probably comes from elephants displaying anxiety over unidentified sounds or movement, such as that caused by mice scurrying around underfoot.

Q —

How do dolphins sleep?

A —

Good question, as all mammals require sleep but dolphins have to be conscious to breath. This means that they cannot go into a full deep sleep, because then they would suffocate! Dolphins have solved this seeming paradox by letting one half of their brain sleep at a time, a fact confirmed by EEG studies. Dolphins sleep about 8 hours day in one of the following fashions:

- swimming slowly and surfacing every now and then for a breath
- resting at the surface with their blowhole exposed
- resting on the bottom (in shallow water) and rising to the surface every now and then to breath.

Q —

Is it true that German Shepherds were renamed Alsatians after World War II?

A —

The German Shepherd was bred originally by a German, Captain Max von Stephanitz, in the late 1800s and early 1900s. His aim was to produce an all-purpose working dog. The correct English name for the breed is 'German Shepherd Dog'. However, in the Allied countries during and after World War II they were called Alsatians to reduce possible association with Germany and the Nazis. The name Alsatian is still commonly used in the UK; it means 'wolf dog'.

Q —

How did the Jack Russell get its name?

A —

The Jack Russell Terrier takes it name from the Reverend John Russell (1795-1883) who bred the terriers for fox hunting. He lived in Devonshire, where he exercised his passion for fox hunting and the breeding of fox hunting dogs.

Q —

How do snakes mate?

A —

The male usually searches for and courts the female when he is ready to mate. Male snakes have two penises called hemipenes (lizards share this attribute). Some snakes alternate between the two and some just use which ever is closest to the female. Some males prevent the female from mating with other males by prolonging mating (remaining connected for up to 6 hours). Others simply hang around for a few days, keeping other males off. Most snakes mate once a year, usually timing it so that the young will emerge when the weather is warm and prey is abundant.

Q —

Is it true that sharks have been around since the time of the dinosaurs?

A —

In fact they were around before the dinosaurs – for more than 300 million years. It is little wonder, as they are supremely adapted to their environment and are some of the best hunters in the world. There are about 350 different types of sharks but researchers think there may be others still to be discovered. Sharks are very healthy creatures. They never get cancer and shark cartilage is currently being used in research to develop anti-cancer drugs.

Q —

What is a baby turkey called and what is the name of the bit of skin that hangs over its beak?

A —

A baby turkey is called a poult. The flap of skin that hangs over a turkey's beak is called a 'snood'. It turns bright read if the turkey gets upset and during courtship. And just for good measure, here are a few more turkey terms for all you Dustin fans:

Gizzard – a part of a bird's stomach that contains tiny stones which help them digest food.

Hen – a female turkey.

Tom – a male turkey; also known as a gobbler.

Wattle – the flap of skin under the turkey's chin. This also turns bright red when the turkey is upset or during courtship.

Chancer – Dustin.

Q –

What is the fastest mammal on earth?

A –

The cheetah is the fastest land mammal, but only over relatively short distances of about 1,800 ft (600m), when it can reach a maximum speed of just over sixty miles per hour. A cheetah can accelerate from 0 to 50 mph in a little under 4 seconds. (Even Jeremy Clarkson should be impressed by that!)

Q —

If someone looks like a horse you might describe them as equine; likewise cow features, bovine or cat-like, feline. If someone looks like a rat, how would you describe them?

A —

You could call them unfortunate but the correct term is murine. And here are a few more gems which you might like to add to your animal lexicon:

bluebird	–	turdine
frog	–	bufotenine
kangaroo	–	macropodine
magpie	–	garruline
ostrich	–	struthious
pig	–	porcine
reptile	–	reptilian or serpentine
skunk	–	mephitine
wombat	–	phascolomian

Q —

What is Ireland's most dangerous animal?

A —

There are no specific statistics. A bull is most likely to inflict potentially fatal injuries but a red deer or badger can be extremely dangerous if cornered.

Q —

What is the collective term for horses?

A —

There are a number of possibilities but the most common term is a 'team' of horses, although the word 'herd' is sometimes used. A number of colts are referred to as a 'rag' and a group of ponies as a 'string'. A number of horses belonging to one owner are a 'stud'. Just take your pick!

Q —

Can you tell me about silverfish?

A —

Silverfish are small, nocturnal, wingless insects. They normally live outside under rocks or leaf mould, in bird nests or ant nests. However, they are also found in homes, where they are considered a pest. They are usually found trapped in the bath or sink but if they find their way into your cereals, or even your clothes, they will feast away. They are also fond of paste and paper. However, they don't have to eat you out of house and home as they can go for as long as a year without eating at all!

Q —

Can animals be homosexual?

A —

Some species of animals do form long-term same-sex relationships. Bottlenose dolphins, which are not known to form heterosexual pair bonds, often form life-long homosexual pairings. Animals which maintain 'bachelor groups', such as bison, gazelle and antelope, commonly form same sex pairs, which last until one of the pair leaves to breed. Homosexuality has also been observed in gorillas, orang-utans, chimpanzees and elephants. Bisexuality is also a feature in some species. Some animals will exhibit a preference for same sex at one stage of life and change preference later. Homosexuality can even be seasonal! Male walruses, for example, often form homosexual pair bonds outside of the breeding season but will revert to heterosexual behaviour during the breeding season.

Jenny once had a homosexual dog called Charlie. (For anyone who is interested his lover's name was Ivor!)

Q —

Do fish have ears?

A —

Not that you can see. Sound vibrations transmit through the fish's body to internal ears which are divided into two sections, the pars superior and the utriculus. The pars superior gives the fish its sense of balance and the utriculus gives the fish its hearing capability.

Q —

Which is the world's largest fish?

A —

It is the whale shark.

Q —

Why are flies attracted to the blue lights in bug zappers?

A —

Unlike humans, flies can see ultraviolet light. This is owing to the complexity of their eyes, which are made up of hundreds of tiny hexagonal lenses. All light sources emit some level of ultraviolet and it is this that the fly is attracted to, mistaking it for sunlight. Insects which are attracted to light are called phototactic.

Q —

What do you call a baby whale?

A —

A baby whale is known as a calf.

Q —

What exactly is cuckoo spit?

A —

Cuckoo spit is a frothy secretion found on plants in the summer months. It is produced by the immature nymph stage of plant lice which in the adult stage are known as froghoppers.

Q —

Which is the biggest bear – I think it's the polar bear?

A —

The polar bear is indeed the largest, weighing up to 1,700 lbs (770 kg). Bears are found in Asia, Europe, North and South America. They vary in size from 3.5 ft to 10 ft (1.1–3 m) in length and the smallest weighs a mere 55 lbs (25 kg). Bears are classified as carnivores but will eat plants, leaves, berries, honey, nuts, roots, insects, fish and small mammals.

The Kodiak bear is a close second. It's a brown bear native to Kodiak Island, Alaska.

Q —

Is it true that greyhounds have the best sight of all dogs?

A —

Probably! The greyhound uses his sense of sight to hunt where other dogs use their sense of smell. He can see small moving objects up to half a mile away. He is certainly the fastest of all dog breeds, being capable of 45 mph sprints. However, he needs far less exercise than most dogs to maintain fitness and has been described as the world's fastest couch potato.

Q —

How long does a chicken have to sit on an egg before it hatches?

A —

Usually around 21 days.

Q —

Do female deer have antlers?

A —

The only type of deer where the female also grows antlers is the reindeer (also known as caribou).

Q —

Can you get twin chickens?

A —

Although you might occasionally crack a double-yolk egg into your breakfast pan, fertilised double-yolk eggs are extremely rare and twin chicks almost never both survive. In a normal, single-yolk egg, the chick has to move around and get its head up to the air cell (the round end). If there are two chicks they will fight each other and usually both die. In a few, rare cases an egg has been deliberately opened at the right time and twin chicks have survived.

Q —

Do dogs laugh?

A —

Researchers in America have recorded 'breathy exhalations', different from standard doggy panting, which could be the canine version of a laugh. This particular sound can trigger playfulness in other dogs and is never observed during aggressive behaviour.

Q —

What is the difference between fur and hair? Why does a dog have hair but a fox has fur?

A —

It seems to just depend on the degree of hairiness! All fur is made up of hair but obviously not all hair is fur. Fur is defined as a soft, dense coat on a hairy mammal.

Q —

How is semen collected from a bull for artificial insemination?

A —

You are not going to believe this! The bulls are kept at artificial insemination studs. The semen is collected by persuading the bull to mount an artificial cow called a mannequin. The mannequin is on four wheels and (here's the best part) there is a person inside! This is not a job for the fainthearted, folks, as the occupant of the mannequin has to place an artificial vagina over the bull's penis in order to collect the semen. Once this brave feat is accomplished the semen is taken to a laboratory where it is examined for numbers and motility (capacity for movement). Depending on these factors, the semen is then diluted between four and ten times and frozen in 'straws'. In this way a single bull can inseminate up to 100,000 cows annually. By the normal method he would be lucky to service one hundred! The use of artificial insemination guarantees high genetic progeny.

Q —

How many toes does an ostrich have?

A —

Two on each foot, four in all.

Q —

Do Great Danes come from Denmark?

A —

That would seem logical, wouldn't it, but the answer is 'no'. Great Danes were originally bred in Germany, where they are called 'deutsche Dogge'.

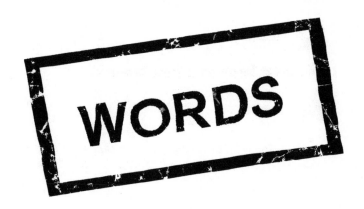

WORDS

What would the world be like without hypothetical situations?

If vegetarians eat vegetables, what do humanitarians eat?

Q —

What exactly does 'the exception that proves the rule' mean?

A —

A very good question as this is a phrase which is often misused in the current vernacular in order to justify an inconsistency. When used in this sense it seems to be saying that the existence of a case that doesn't follow a rule proves that the rule applies in all other cases and so is generally correct. This is obviously nonsense, since the logical implication of finding that something doesn't follow a rule is that there must be something wrong with the rule!

The origin of the phrase is in a mediaeval legal principle: *exceptio probat regulam in casibus non exceptis*, which roughly translates as 'the exception confirms the rule in the cases not excepted'. For example, if you drive down a street where notices read 'Parking prohibited Monday to Saturday', you may reasonably infer that parking is allowed on Sundays. A sign on a nightclub door which says 'Entry free before

10pm' implies that entry is not free after 10pm. So, in its strict sense, the principle is arguing that the existence of an allowed exception to a rule reaffirms the existence of the rule. Got it?

Q —

Why do people say 'excuse my French' when they use bad language?

A —

For centuries the poor old French have been stereotyped by English-speakers as permissive and less likely to be offended by obscenity. The phrases 'Excuse my French' or 'Pardon my French' became popular about a hundred years ago as an apology for swearing or using some form of obscenity in polite company. The phrase first appeared in *Harper's Magazine* in 1895. It is still used today when a speaker feels his listeners might be offended by his choice of language. It is thought that the term 'French' was employed in this sense as it already had a history of association with things considered vulgar. As far back as the early 16th century 'French pox' and 'the French disease' were synonyms for genital herpes and 'French-sick' was another term for syphilis. Various dictionaries still equate the adjective French with 'spiciness' or 'slight impropriety', as in French letter for 'condom', French kiss and French (i.e. 'sexually explicit') novels.

Q —

How was the term 'fifth column' coined?

A —

A fifth column refers to an organised body in sympathy with and working for the enemy within a country at war. The phrase was first employed by General Emilio Mola Vidal, a Nationalist general during the Spanish Civil War (1936-39). As four of his army columns moved on the besieged city of Madrid, the general referred to his militant supporters within the capital as his 'fifth column', intent on undermining the loyalist government from within.

Q —

Where does the delightful expression 'I'll have your guts for garters' come from?

A —

This phrase has been around in various forms since the eighteenth century. When it first came into use it would have implied the threat of disembowelling (a most extreme form of judicial punishment!) but in modern times it simply implies that one will take some unspecified action in reprisal for unacceptable behaviour. It is a phrase employed by NCOs to intimidate new recruits (in the movies, anyway!). The fact that virtually nobody wears garters anymore has not affected the popularity of this alliterative and graphic threat.

Q —

Would you know the origin of 'heebie-jeebies' to describe a state of nervous depression or anxiety?

A —

It is almost certain that it was invented by the American cartoonist Billy De Beck. It first appeared in one of his Barney Google cartoons in the *New York American* on 26 October 1923. At that time it was spelt heeby-jeeby. The phrase seems to have no origin other than De Beck's fevered imagination.

Q —

Where does the expression 'to kick the bucket' come from?

A —

The most plausible theory is that the 'bucket' in question was originally the French word *buque*, meaning a yoke or similar piece of wood. This term applied in particular to the beam from which a pig was hung for slaughtering. Inevitably the poor pig would struggle during the process and would 'kick the buque'. The term bucket is still used in parts of Norfolk, England, for the beam on which a slaughtered pig is hung.

Q —

Why is a Mexican Wave so called?

A —

The wave effect that is formed when the crowd in a sports stadium rise up and down from their seats in succession was first dubbed 'the Mexican Wave' during the soccer World Cup in Mexico in 1986. It had been witnessed in US colleges in earlier times but Mexico '86 brought it to a mass audience for the first time. It is a great way for the crowd to create their own entertainment if a game is a bit pedestrian – or to celebrate if their team is winning!

Q —

What is the origin of the expression to 'pay through the nose'?

A —

This is yet another popular expression whose origins are uncertain. It is possible that it goes back as far as the Vikings who, according to legend, would slice people's noses open if they failed to pay an acceptable ransom or tribute. This explanation probably owes more to legend than to fact, however, as the earliest recorded use of the expression in English dates from the 17th century. A more plausible theory is that a person who didn't repay a debt on time was likely to get a punch on the nose and thereby pay in blood. To this day the phrase is still associated with a degree of extortion, invariably implying overcharging.

Q —

I recently came across the word 'slubberdegullion' as a term of abuse. Can you tell me anything more about it?

A —

This is an archaic term meaning a 'slovenly, worthless fellow'. It could also be spelt 'slabberdegullion'. It is one of any amazing array of disparaging terms which have been lost to the English language over time. Read aloud the following extract from Sir Thomas Urquhart's (1653) translation of Rabelais' *Gargantua and Pantagruel* to get an idea of how impoverished the language of abuse has become:

The bun-sellers or cake-makers were in nothing inclinable to their request; but, which was worse, did injure them most outrageously, called them prattling gabblers, lickorous gluttons, freckled bittors, mangy rascals, shite-a-bed scoundrels, drunken roysters, sly knaves, drowsy loiterers, slapsauce fellows, slabberdegullion druggels, lubberly louts, cozening foxes, ruffian rogues, paltry customers, sycophant-varlets, drawlatch hoydens, flouting milksops, jeering companions, staring clowns, forlorn snakes, ninny lobcocks, scurvy sneaksbies, fondling fops, base loons, saucy coxcombs, idle lusks, scoffing braggarts, noddy meacocks, blockish grutnols, doddipol-joltheads, jobbernol goosecaps, foolish loggerheads, flutch calf-lollies, grouthead gnat-snappers, lob-dotterels, gaping changelings, codshead loobies, woodcock slangams, ninny-hammer flycatchers, noddypeak simpletons, turdy gut, shitten shepherds, and other suchlike defamatory epithets.

You don't even need to know what the half of these mean – their sound alone leaves you in no doubt that you are hearing insults of the highest order!

Q —

What is kilter?

A —

Kilter means good working order or condition. It is a variant of the seventeenth century word 'kelter' whose origin is unknown. If something is 'out of kilter' it is not working as it should.

Q —

What do the initials L.E. stand for on Irish naval ships?

A —

They stand for *long eireann*, Irish boat.

Q —

Where does the saying 'three sheets to the wind' come from?

A —

The phrase dates back to the early 1800s. The 'sheet' refers to the rope or chain at the lower corner of a sail, which regulates its position. To have a sheet loose in the wind is bad seamanship. To have three loose means you have lost control of the vessel. Thus, 'three sheets to the wind' has come to mean out of control through the demon drink.

Q —

What is the origin of the term 'hustings'?

A —

The term 'hustings' today refers to any electioneering activity. However, before the days of mass communication, the hustings were platforms from which parliamentary candidates were nominated and addressed the electorate. The word derives from the Old Norse *húsping*, meaning a royal council.

Q —

Where does the phrase 'on cloud nine' come from?

A —

This phrase is usually attributed to the U.S. Weather Bureau, who used to describe clouds by an arithmetic sequence. Level Nine described the highest cumulonimbus, which can be as high as 40,000 ft (11,750m). The phrase has been around since the 1930s. It has the same meaning as 'in seventh heaven', which comes from a Danish expression.

Q —

What does it mean if you call someone Bohemian?

A —

It refers to someone with an unconventional lifestyle, often an artist or writer, who lives outside the accepted mores of society. The term dates from the mid-nineteenth century and derives from the association of an unconventional lifestyle with the Romany gypsies of Bohemia. Interestingly, Bohemians Football Club are nicknamed 'The Gypsies'.

Q —

What does 'sic' mean after a line of print?

A —

It means 'thus (used or spelt)', indicating that what precedes it is written intentionally or copied verbatim, even though it may appear to be incorrect.

Q —

Where does the word 'shrapnel' come from?

A —

The term shrapnel can refer to fragments of a bomb thrown out by its explosion but its true and original meaning comes from a delightful invention by the nineteenth-century British general, Henry Shrapnel. Shrapnel's invention was a hollow projectile containing bullets or pieces of metal, timed to burst slightly short of its objective and thus showering its lethal contents.

Q —

What is the opposite of misogynist?

A —

Well, a misogynist is somebody who hates all women so the opposite would be somebody who loves all women – that would be a philogynist. However, if you are looking for a word to describe a man-hater, most dictionaries don't give one, but taking the same Greek roots as misogynist leads some lexicons to list 'misandrist' as one who hates all men.

Q —

Why is there an 'r' in 'mrs'?

A —

Because it is actually a contraction of 'mistress'.

Q —

Is a tissue called 'a tissue' because when we sneeze we go 'a-tissue'?

A —

No, that's not the reason. The word comes originally from the Latin *texere* and the Old French *tistre*, meaning 'to weave'.

Q —

What do you call a place where bees are kept – not a hive?

A —

The general term for a place where bees are kept is 'apiary'.

Q —

Can you explain the saying 'raise (sic) to the ground' – it doesn't make sense to me?

A —

The phrase is actually 'raze to the ground'. To raze means to completely destroy or to level to the ground a building or a settlement. It is also a great way to use up the 'z' if you get caught with it in Scrabble!

Q —

What does 'hand over fist' mean?

A —

The expression originally was 'hand over hand' and referred to nautical work such as rope climbing or pulling something in by means of a rope. Over time it came to mean 'continuous progress' or 'regular advances' and would have been used if a chasing ship was gaining on another. It was a small step from this to today's meaning of 'speedily, increasingly'. Virtually the only way in which the phrase is now used is 'making money hand over fist'.

Q —

Where does the word monopoly come from?

A —

Monopoly means the exclusive control of the supply of a commodity or service. It comes via Latin, *monopolium* (one seller), from the Greek *monopólion*.

Q —

Why is a crowbar called a crowbar?

A —

It is so called because the flattened end resembles a crow's foot — doesn't it?

Q —

What does 'logistical' mean on the side of articulated trucks?

A —

This is a relatively modern word which refers to the planning and management of how things are moved, particularly in relation to the military or industrial goods. It has a secondary meaning, that of planning and managing any complex task.

Q —

What did Little Miss Muffet sit on?

A —

It was a tuffet. It is a sixteenth century word meaning a small mound or clump of grass, or a low seat or stool.

Q —

What is the correct definition of a gazebo?

A —

It is an eighteenth-century word which originally related to any structure, including balconies and turrets, which commanded a pleasant view. In more recent times it has come to mean a small building, usually slightly elevated and open-sided, commanding a good view.

Q —

When you buy a new car why does everyone say 'well wear'?

A —

It expresses the hope that the item you have purchased with give good service, i.e. will not wear out too quickly. The term used to be applied to new clothing but in recent times has been attached to a variety of new acquisitions, most notably cars.

Q —

What does the abbreviation 'cons' stand for in 'all mod cons'?

A —

This is estate agent speak for 'all modern conveniences'. It is probably a bit outdated nowadays but was commonly used when central heating, dishwashers and broadband connections were not taken for granted!

Q —

Why was the phrase 'hocus pocus' adopted by magicians?

A —

It is actually a seventeenth-century contraction of a pseudo-Latin phrase used by conjurers and magicians to impress their audiences. They would bluster '*hax pax max deus adimax*'.

Q —

Where did the name Fitzpatrick come from and has it any connection to Saint Patrick?

A —

This is a tricky one because the prefix 'Fitz' is Norman French for 'son of' but Fitzpatrick is an Anglicisation of MacGiolla Phadraig, meaning 'son of the servant of St Patrick'. The original Giolla Phadraig was the tenth-century ruler of the ancient kingdom of Upper Ossory, including parts of present day Laois and Kilkenny. The name was Anglicised in the early sixteenth century when the chief of the family accepted the title of Lord Baron of Upper Ossory from Henry VIII. Although the surname is now widespread throughout Ireland the

largest concentration of Fitzpatricks is still in
County Laois.

Q —

What is it called if you can't pronounce your 'Rs'?

A —

It is called lallation.

Q —

**What does the 'rag' in a university rag week
stand for? I was told it meant 'raise a grand'.**

A —

It sounds possible but most of our sources
indicate that rag stands for 'raise and give' – it
has a more noble ring, don't you think?

Q —

Where does the word 'quiz' come from?

A —

It is possibly a corruption of the Latin '*qui es*', meaning 'who are you?' or of the English dialect verb *quiset*, meaning to question. Either way its root is in the inquisitive.

That's the boring truth. There is a spurious Irish connection which is untrue but more interesting. The story goes that a Dublin theatre owner called Richard Daly made a bet with one of his mates that he could, within forty-eight hours, make a nonsense word known throughout the city of Dublin. He got the staff of his theatre to write the word 'quiz' on walls around the city. The next day the strange word was on everybody's lips and became part of the language. Great story, but unfortunately the word 'quiz' can be found in publications prior to Daly's supposed bet.

Q —

Why are two weeks called a fortnight?

A —

This one is very straightforward. It comes from

the Old English *feowetine niht*, which means 'fourteen nights'.

Q —

American coins are called cents but in the movies they are often referred to as pennies – are they known as pennies?

A —

Yes, in America and Canada the one cent coin is commonly called a penny.

Q —

Why do people say 'that's a different kettle of fish' – what has a kettle to do with fish?

A —

A kettle was originally any deep pan for boiling food. A fish kettle is a large, oval saucepan with a handle at each end, large enough to take a salmon lengthways. 'A different kettle of fish' means a different matter or a whole new ball game whereas 'a pretty kettle of fish' means an awkward state of affairs or a messy predicament.

The latter derives from the eighteenth-century Scottish custom of picnicking on boiled salmon (cooked in kettles, of course) – gatherings that sometimes became unruly affairs.

Q —

My gran used to say 'you look like the wreck of the Hesperus' if someone was a bit the worse for wear. Any idea where it comes from?

A —

The saying comes from the title of a poem by Henry Wadsworth Longfellow (1807-1882), *The Wreck of the Hesperus*. In twenty-two verses it tells the story of the ill-fated *Hesperus*, smashed on the 'Reef of Norman's Woe' by a hurricane because its arrogant master ignores the warnings of an old, weather-wise sailor.

Q —

Why do people say 'daft as a brush' – how silly are brushes?

A —

The best explanation we could find dates back to the awful Victorian practice of using small children as chimney sweeps. The children had to work their way up the chimney ahead of the sweep's brushes, clearing blockages by hand. Many children suffered head injuries – some were even pushed head-first down chimneys – and as a result became brain-damaged.

Q —

Where does the word coleslaw come from?

A —

Take your pick! Some sources give the origin as Dutch, from the words *kool* (cabbage) and *sla* (salad). Others give Old Norse or Old High German origins. Don't think, just eat.

Q —

Where did the word 'bootleg' come from?

A —

It is believed to have come from the illegal sale of alcohol to native Americans in the days of the Wild West. The sellers would transport the alcohol by strapping flat bottles of liquor to their legs. The term became popular during the years of Prohibition in the US and is mostly associated with that time.

Q —

What is a redeye?

A —

A redeye usually refers to a long-haul flight with an early morning arrival. In this part of the world that is most often a transatlantic flight west to east, which leaves travellers literally red-eyed. The term also refers to the common photographic phenomenon, occurring with simple flash cameras, which gives the subject red pupils. A third, less common meaning which we found was 'cheap whiskey'.

Q —

Where does the expression 'getting the bum's rush' come from?

A —

The bum in question refers to a tramp or vagrant. The rush, or rushes, were the sweeping end of a broom. If a tramp arrived at an inhospitable inn or home he would be chased away with the aid of a broom.

Why was the Lone Ranger called 'lone' when Tonto was always hanging around?

What colour does a Smurf turn if you choke it?

Q —

Were there really only twelve episodes of *Fawlty Towers*?

A —

Yes indeed. There were two seasons of six programmes on BBC2. The first season was originally shown in 1975 and the second in 1979. *Fawlty Towers* was written by John Cleese and his wife, Connie Booth. They had divorced before the second season began but the break-up of their marriage had no adverse effects on the brilliant writing.

The twelve episodes are:

Series One
1 A Touch of Class
2 The Builders
3 The Wedding Party
4 The Hotel Inspectors
5 Gourmet Night
6 The Germans

Series Two
1 Communications Problems
2 The Psychiatrist

Q —

What's the breed of Hagrid's dog in the *Harry Potter* films?

A —

It is a Neapolitan Mastiff.

Q —

Do you remember Catweazle? What was the name of his pet frog?

A —

Of course I'm too young to have any but the haziest memories of Catweazle but scrupulous research has reminded me that he was an eleventh-century magician who travelled through time to the twentieth century. His companion was actually a toad whose name was Touchwood.

Q —

What was the name of the park ranger in *Yogi Bear*?

A —

Ranger Smith.

Q —

Was the actor who voiced Troy McClure in *The Simpsons* murdered by his wife?

A —

Yes, in 1998 Phil Hartman was shot by his wife who then turned the gun on herself. He voiced a number of characters in *The Simpsons*, including Troy McClure and Lionel Hutz.

Q —

Who wrote *War of the Worlds* and who did the narration in the original radio broadcast way back when?

A —

H.G. (Herbert George) Wells wrote *The War of the Worlds* in 1898. The book is about a Martian invasion of earth and is considered one of the greatest science fiction novels. In 1938 Orson Welles directed and narrated a radio adaptation of the book. To heighten the drama, Welles decided to present the story as a news report. The production was so realistic that there was panic across the USA. Some people took to the roads, others hid in cellars and some wrapped their heads in wet towels to protect themselves from poisonous Martian gas!

Q —

Who played Bishop Brennan in *Father Ted*?

A —

The man you are looking for is James (Jim) Norton.

Q —

Is it true that the Americans are making a version of *Father Ted*?

A —

It is rumoured that this is to happen. Steve Martin will play Father Ted and Graham Norton will play Father Dougal. The show will be set on a small, fictional island off New York.

Q —

Was Ronald Reagan considered for the Humphrey Bogart part in *Casablanca*?

A —

Yes, Ronald Reagan was in fact Warner Brothers' first choice for the part of Rick Blaine. Luckily he was otherwise engaged!

Q —

Did *Star Trek* feature the first interracial TV kiss?

A —

Yes, in the episode 'Plato's Stepchildren' Uhura and Captain Kirk were forced to kiss by their captors. Because the scene was potentially controversial it was decided to keep a safety net and shoot it with and without the kiss. However, William Shatner (Kirk) had other ideas and kept kissing until there was time for just one more take. When the director called for action Shatner crossed his eyes and so the take was unusable and the scene was broadcast, kiss and all, making television history.

Q —

Is a movie only a prequel if it is made after the original?

A —

Yes, a prequel is defined as a film or novel set at a time preceding the action of an existing work.

Q —

Is there going to be a *Simpsons* movie?

A —

It is reported that Matt Groening and James L Brooks are developing a film script but the finished product will not be seen until at least 2006.

Q —

Is it true that Madonna has made sixteen films?

A —

Madonna has actually made eighteen movies.
They are:

Desperately Seeking Susan	1985
Vision Quest	1985
A Certain Sacrifice	1985
Shanghai Surprise	1986
Who's That Girl?	1987
Bloodhounds on Broadway	1989
Dick Tracy	1990
Shadows and Fog	1992
A League of Their Own	1992
Body of Evidence	1993
Dangerous Games	1993
Blue in the Face	1995
Four Rooms	1995
Girl 16	1996
Evita	1996
Next Best Thing	2002
Die Another Day (cameo role)	2002
Swept Away	2003

Q —

Was Tim Robbins in the film *Top Gun*?

A —

Yes, he played Lieutenant Sam 'Merlin' Wells.

Q —

What was the very last line spoken in the final episode of *Cheers*?

A —

In the final episode Sam and Diane are on the point of getting married when he decides that he is not the marrying kind and is happiest behind the bar. The very last scene is of a mysterious man coming to the door of the bar and Sam saying, 'We're closed'.

Who was that man? I don't know – but that wasn't the question!

Q —

Why do American radio stations all have names like WYKY, etc?

A —

In the earliest days of radio blocks of initial letters were assigned to different countries as their call letters. After the London International Radiotelegraph Conference of 1912 the letters W, K, N and A were assigned to the US. The letters W and K were used to designate commercial broadcasters and N and A were allocated to military users of radio. The first US radio stations were allowed to select their own three- or four-letter call sign, beginning with either a W or a K. In the late 1920s the system was formalised by the Federal Radio Commission and all stations were required to use a four-letter combination. Additionally, stations east of the Mississippi were compelled to used an initial W and stations west of the Mississippi were required to use an initial K.

Q —

What is the relevance of the numbers beside each programme in the TV listings in the newspapers and TV guides?

A —

The numbers allow you to access a quick record system for VCRs. If your video recorder has VideoPlus you can simply key in the number of the programme you wish to record and the machine will automatically record on the correct channel at the correct time (even if the programme is delayed for some reason).

Q —

What was the first talkie?

A —

The first talking feature film was *The Jazz Singer* (1927), starring Al Jolson.

Q —

What was the name of the painting in the *Mr Bean* film?

A —

The portrait was Whistler's Mother painted, not surprisingly, by James Abbott McNeill Whistler (1834-1903), an American painter and etcher. The film in which it featured was *Bean – The Ultimate Disaster Movie*.

If one synchronised swimmer drowns, do they all have to?

Why do we have a tourist season if we're not allowed to shoot them?

Q —

Who is Aung San Suu Kyi?

A —

Daw Aung San Suu Kyi has been the figurehead for Myanmar's (formerly Burma) struggle for democracy since 1988. She was born on June 19th 1945, and was the daughter of Burma's independence hero, Aung San. Her father was assassinated when she was only two years old. Aung San Suu Kyi was educated in Burma, India, and the United Kingdom.

In 1988 she returned to Burma from London to nurse her dying mother and was plunged into a nationwide uprising which had just begun. Joining the newly-formed National League for Democracy, Suu Kyi began calling for freedom and democracy. The military regime responded to the uprising with brute force, killing thousands of demonstrators in a matter of months. However, the regime was eventually forced to call a general election in 1990.

While campaigning for the NLD, Suu Kyi and many others were detained by the regime.

She was placed under house arrest and has been in and out of detention ever since. Despite this, the NLD went on to win a staggering 82% of the seats in parliament but the regime never recognised the results.

Suu Kyi has won numerous international awards, including the Nobel Peace Prize, the Sakharov Prize from the European Parliament, the United States Presidential Medal of Freedom, and the Jawaharlal Nehru Award from India.

Q —

How many Nobel prizes are awarded each year?

A —

Nobel prizes are awarded in six categories: chemistry, physics, economics, physiology or medicine, peace-campaigning and literature.

Q —

How did Houdini die?

A —

Harry Houdini, the great escapologist, was born Ehrich Weiss in Budapest in 1874. His parents emigrated to the U.S.A. when Harry was very young and settled in Appleton, Wisconsin. Harry started his career as a trapeze artist but eventually became world famous for his feats of magic and escapology. He was also well-known for his debunking of fraudulent psychics and mediums.

There is a popular misconception that Harry died after an escape bid went wrong but this is probably the legacy of a 1953 movie *Houdini*, starring Tony Curtis. In the movie, Houdini dies during a failed escape from the infamous Chinese Water Torture Cell. The truth is less dramatic; the poor man died from peritonitis resulting from a burst appendix in 1926.

Q —

Who is the richest person in the world?

A —

There really is no contest. Bill Gates (Mr Microsoft) is the world's richest person by a considerable margin. He was the world's first $100 billion man and, if his wealth continues to grow at the 61 per cent compound annual rate it has enjoyed so far, he will become the world's first trillionaire, worth $1,000,000,000,000. Apart from his 21% stake in Microsoft he owns several other companies and is the major shareholder in a $9 billion satellite venture. Bill Gates's personal fortune now exceeds the economic output of all but the 18 wealthiest nations and is likely to overtake the gross national product of the UK.

And, don't forget, this is the guy who dropped out of Harvard!

Q —

Which presidents' faces are carved into Mount Rushmore?

A —

One of the most iconic of American images, the carvings on Mount Rushmore in South Dakota are as high as a five-storey building. The four heads are those of Presidents Washington, Jefferson, Roosevelt and Lincoln.

Q —

Was the real Zorro Irish?

A —

To the sceptic it would sometimes appear that we will lay claim to any heroic figure, real or fictional! However, it does seem that there may be some truth to the legend of an Irish Zorro!

The twentieth-century hero of comic books and films was the creation of Johnson McCulley and first appeared in August 1919 as a serial in a journal entitled *All-Story Weekly*. Zorro subsequently appeared in numerous silent and talking movies. But the intriguing roots of the legend of Zorro go back much further, to 1615 in County Wexford. Here was born William

Lamport, a Catholic who fled his native country and the oppression of Cromwell's Commonwealth. In 1643 he enlisted in one of three Irish regiments in Spanish service and eventually found his way to the Spanish colony of Mexico. At about this time he took the name Guillen Lombardo.

In Mexico he lived amongst the native Indians, studying astrology and their healing skills. He developed a great sympathy for the native Mexicans and became a leader of the fledgling Mexican independence movement. These activities brought him to the notice of the Spanish Inquisition and he was eventually arrested and accused of conspiracy against Spain and its Most Catholic Majesty. Guillen was jailed for 10 years, but escaped from his dungeon and took to daubing the walls of Mexico City with his name and anti-Spanish graffiti by night. However, he was arrested again in 1652 when found in bed with the wife of the Spanish Viceroy to Mexico (he certainly knew how to push his luck!). He was sentenced to 7 years imprisonment, at the end of which he was handed over to the Inquisition to be burnt at the stake as a heretic. The legend goes that

William/Guillen/Zorro was tied to the stake in Mexico City in 1659 but, as the bundles of kindling were lit, he undid the ropes that bound him and strangled himself before the flames could reach him.

Q —

Why is Sting called Sting?

A —

There are several legends but the most common, and the most plausible, is that he acquired the nickname whilst in a band called the Phoenix Jazzmen. He took to wearing a black and yellow striped top which made him look like a big bee. Hence the nickname, 'Sting'.

Q —

Was Sherlock Holmes a real person?

A —

No, although it is a popular misconception that he was. He and his faithful sidekick, Dr Watson, were the inventions of Sir Arthur Conan Doyle.

Q —

Could it be true that Winston Churchill won a Nobel Prize?

A —

He did indeed. In 1953 he won the Nobel Prize for Literature. He received his knighthood in the same year.

Q —

Who are TOFOG?

A —

TOFOG are Thirty Odd Foot Of Grunts, an Australian band fronted by Russell Crowe.

Q —

Is it true that the chef, Gordon Ramsay, used to be a professional footballer?

A —

Yes. The celebrity chef, now more famous for his colourful language than his footballing skills, played for Oxford United as a teenager. There he was spotted by a scout for Glasgow Rangers and was signed by the Scottish team at the age of fifteen. Within three years, however, he had given up football to take a Higher National Diploma in Hotel Management. The rest, as they say, is history.

Q —

How did Barry White die?

A —

Barry White died on 4th July 2003 from kidney failure, after suffering from high blood pressure for many years. He was 58.

Q —

Whatever happened to the little girl who played 'Annie' in the film of the same name?

A —

Aileen Quinn was chosen to star in the 1982 film from a field of 8,000 girls! She starred in one further film, *The Frog Prince*, which was a video only release. Her main career has been on the musical stage, where she works to this day. In 1995 she toured with *Fiddler on the Roof* and in 1998 she worked in a Broadway production of *Peter Pan*.

Q —

Everybody knows who was the first man on the moon but who was the last?

A —

The last manned mission to the moon was Apollo 17 and the last man to set foot there was Gene Cernan. His comments on leaving the moon are not as famous as Neil Armstrong's 'one small step . . .' but, for the record, here they are: 'As we leave the moon at Taurus Littrow, we leave as we came and, God willing, as we shall return, with peace and hope for all mankind. Godspeed the crew of Apollo 17.'

Q —

Could you please tell my friends that Bob Geldof has not been knighted by the Queen? He is Irish.

A —

Sorry, but you will have to climb down on this one. Bob Geldof has received many awards in recognition of his work for famine relief in the Third World, amongst them an honorary knighthood from Queen Elizabeth II. He is officially a KBE, a Knight of the Most Excellent Order of the British Empire. As a non-British subject, he was precluded from receiving a full knighthood and the title 'Sir'. However, this doesn't stop people referring to him as 'Sir Bob'.

Q —

What is Mr T's real name?

A —

The bejewelled star of *The A-Team* was born Laurence Tureaud.

Q —

What was President Mary McAleese's maiden name?

A —

She was born Mary Patricia Leneghan on 27th June 1951 in Belfast.

Q —

Is it true that Oliver Cromwell once cancelled Christmas?

A —

Cromwell was a big believer in solemnity and hated all the partying that went along with Christmas. He believed that the day should be acknowledged only by sermons and prayer services. To this end, the British Parliament officially abolished the celebration of Christmas in 1643. Apparently nobody paid a lot of attention to this as Cromwell had another go at banning the yuletide festival in 1649 when he outlawed Christmas carols! The Puritans in America also tried to take the fun out of Christmas and promoted Thanksgiving Day as the major annual festival.

Q —

Is the story of the *Marie Celeste* fact or fiction?

A —

The *Marie Celeste*, a two-masted sailing ship, left New York harbour on 5th November 1872. She was bound for Genoa, Italy, with a cargo of industrial alcohol. One month later she was found drifting in the Atlantic, between the Portuguese coast and the Azores. When she was boarded there was no sign of the crew, but breakfast was laid on the table and valuables were still locked in the safe. However, the ship's only lifeboat, sextant, chronometer and logbook were all missing. No-one knows what became of the ten people on board or why they apparently abandoned ship in such haste.

Q —

I heard that Christina Aguilera's mother was from Mayo. Is this true?

A —

According to our research she was actually from Wexford and her maiden name was Kearns.

Q —

Where was Steve Finnan born?

A —

Steve Finnan, Irish international defender, was born in Limerick on 24th April 1976.

Q —

Is Colin Farrell Irish?

A —

With a name like that?! Colin Farrell was born and raised in Castleknock in Dublin. He is the son of former footballer, Eamonn Farrell, and nephew of Tommy Farrell, and both of them played for Shamrock Rovers in the 1960s. Colin was at the Gaiety School of Drama when he was offered his first professional role in the mini-series *Falling for a Dancer*. After that he moved to *Ballykissangel*. His big breakthrough came with his part in the movie *Tigerland* in which he played a rough Texan.

FOOD & DRINK

They say an onion is the only vegetable that can make you cry – did you ever get a belt from a turnip?

Q —

What is the significance of 57 in 'Heinz 57 Varieties'?

A —

In 1896, Henry John Heinz noticed an advertisement for '21 styles of shoes'. He decided that his own products were not styles but varieties. Although he had many more than 57 foods in production at the time, the numbers 5 and 7 held special significance for himself and his wife. Thus he adopted the slogan '57 Varieties' and one of the most enduring and well-known advertising slogans of all time was born.

Q —

Did the Italians invent pasta?

A —

As with many everyday things, the true origins of pasta are lost in the mists of time! Foods made with flour and water were certainly a part of early Roman, Sicilian, and Greek diets and these would have been some of the first forms of pasta. Certainly, over the centuries, the Italians have turned pasta making into an art form, developing hundreds of shapes, sizes, colours, and textures. To accompany these they have also created an amazing array of sauces, using basic ingredients such as tomatoes, cheese, cream, butter, olive oil, sweet basil, oregano, garlic and any number of vegetables. So the next time you are enjoying lasagne, penne, tagliatelle, spaghetti – or any other pasta – remember to toast Italian imagination!

Q —

What do you call the white of an egg?

A —

Albumen.

Q —

Is it dangerous to eat fourteen chewing gums five days a week?

A —

Not really, but be warned, most chewing gums bear a cautionary note to the effect that they contain a source of phenylalanine, excessive consumption of which may produce laxative effects!

Q —

Where did sandwiches originate?

A —

Credit is usually given to John Montagu, the 4th Earl of Sandwich. Whilst involved in a marathon gambling session in or around 1762 he requested that his meat be served between two pieces of bread so that the game would not be interrupted by a formal meal.

Q —

Are the green bits on potatoes poisonous?

A —

When potatoes are exposed to light they begin to turn green, indicating the presence of solanine, a poisonous alkaloid. The concentrations of solanine in modern potatoes would never be enough to cause harm, unlike those available in earlier centuries when eating green spuds could bring a body out in a very unpleasant rash.

Q —

Why do onions make you cry?

A —

Why you cut into an onion it releases a sulphurous, upwardly mobile gas. When this gas comes into contact with the water always present in your eyelids it produces sulphuric acid. Your eyes will blink and produce tears as a reflex action to flush out the offending agent.

Q —

Is there such an implement as a 'spork' – a cross between a spoon and a fork?

A —

Apparently, yes. This is the utensil favoured by a number of American fast-food outlets. It has tines, like a fork, and a bowl, like a spoon.

Q —

What are the ingredients of a 'Red Witch' drink?

A —

The ingredients are Pernod, blackcurrant, cider and ice. Put the required amount of ice into a pint glass; add a double Pernod and a splash of blackcurrant (for colour); fill with cider.

Q —

Is there really much iron in a pint of Guinness?

A —

If you are drinking it to raise your iron levels you will need an awful lot! The RDA (Recommended Daily Allowance) of iron for men is 11mg and for women 14mg; the iron content of a pint of Guinness is 0.3mg! Compare this with some other readily available foods:

2 Weetabix	4.5mg
100g prunes	3.4mg
1 lamb chop	1.9mg
1 egg	1.1mg

Q —

Is it true that it takes four days to digest a banana?

A —

If fruit is eaten on an empty stomach it takes very little time to digest – about 20 minutes to an hour. Bananas are actually the slowest, taking 45 minutes to an hour to digest, but certainly not several days. If you eat fruit after a meal it can make you feel uncomfortable because it will start to ferment on top of the more slowly digesting foods you have already eaten.

Q —

The new advertisements for 'going to the pub' are sponsored by Diageo. Who or what is Diageo?

A —

Diageo is a multinational company which was formed in 1997 by the merger of GrandMet and Guinness.

Q —

Is Buckfast really made by monks?

A —

Buckfast Tonic Wine has been made at Buckfast Abbey in England since the 1880s. The recipe is attributed to French monks who settled there. They imported base wines from Spain and added their own tonic ingredients. If you want to sample the stuff in its birthplace, Buckfast is open to visitors – you can even stay in a guesthouse. They welcome almost half-a-million visitors every year.

Q –

What's the difference between brandy and cognac?

A –

Cognac is a brandy which comes from the Cognac region of France. The area is noted for its special distillation process as well as its soil and climate, considered ideal for brandy production. Brandy distilled outside of this region cannot be called Cognac. In short, all Cognac is brandy but not all brandy is Cognac!

Q –

What is the difference between beer and lager?

A —

As with the previous question, the answer is that all lagers are beers but not all beers are lagers! Lagers originated in Germany and Bohemia and were brewed for keeping (there's a novel concept). They are typically a light-coloured beer brewed with a low proportion of hops.

Q —

What was the first breakfast cereal?

A —

The very first breakfast cereal was produced in 1892 and it was Shredded Wheat. This was quickly followed by Dr John Kellogg's Cornflakes in 1894.

Q —

Is cod liver oil really the oil from the liver of a cod fish?

A —

Yes. Cod liver oil is obtained from the livers of cod and other similar fish. It is a good source of vitamins A and D and omega-3 essential fatty acid.

Q —

Is it just a myth that oily fish is good for your brain?

A —

On the contrary, more and more research is indicating that the essential fatty acids in oily fish and other foods are vital to brain function. Oily fish such as salmon, sardines, trout, herring and mackerel, as well as olive and flax seed oils, are good sources of DHA, an omega-3 fatty acid which is one of the primary building blocks of the brain. It plays a major role in how quickly the brain functions. It has been linked to visual ability and especially to optimal memory function. Omega-3 fatty acids have also been shown to have beneficial effects on the heart.

Q —

What's the difference between pesto and anti-pesto?

A —

This question is actually based on a small spelling mistake! Antipasto is an Italian appetizer. It may be a selection of cooked meats and sausages, marinated fish, a selection of vegetables or any other combination of foods. Pesto, on the other hand, has come to mean a richly flavoured paste, usually used with pasta, made from puréed herbs and vegetables. The classic, original recipe for pesto includes crushed pine nuts, garlic, basil, olive oil and parmesan cheese.

Why does the other queue always move faster?

Is it true that the clinical name for Viagra is mycoxafloppin?

Q —

Where do all the odd socks go?

A —

Answer provided by Shane Ward:

Where do all the odds socks go?
It drives me to despair.
No matter how I wash the things
One goes to, who knows where?
Ten socks inside a pillowcase
And all of them are mine.
I pull them out once they are washed
To count them. Yep. There's nine!
What is it with these wash machines?
I wish that it would stop.
So many socks I've lost in there
I could have filled a shop.
And why just socks for heaven sake?
It simply goes too far
I never lose a shirt, or vest,
nor underpants or bra.
Could the thing be eating them?
No. Somehow I think not.
Nor is it some strange payment

Like a laundromat type slot.
I wonder what would happen
If the day should come
That in the wash machine I put
Not two socks - only one?
And if I sit by that machine
And guard it like a sentry
Would I be surprised to find
The metal barrel empty?
Oh where do all the odd socks go?
I'll never understand
The only way I'll keep them all
Is wash the things by hand!

Q —

Why do dark colours absorb more heat than lighter colours?

A —

It's true, a navy shirt hanging out in the sun will dry faster than a similar white shirt and here's why. All objects absorb radiation (energy) and light is a form of radiation. When white, pure light falls on an object, that object absorbs some of the light and reflects some of the light. When all the light incident on the object is reflected we see white. When all the light incident is absorbed we see the object as colourless (black). So scientifically black is not a colour; it is the absence of all colour. As radiation is energy, the greater the amount of light absorbed the more it will heat an object. White absorbs the least energy and will be heated the least. Pale colours have more white in them and hence they too reflect most of the light falling on them. The opposite happens for dark colours. They absorb the most energy and hence get heated more quickly. So if you don't want to rely on the tumble-dryer, just buy black clothes!

Q —

Does petrol freeze?

A —

Petrol should freeze if you get it cold enough. However, petrol does not consist of a single kind of molecule – it contains several different hydrocarbons (molecules consisting of hydrogen and carbon atoms), which freeze at different rates over a range of temperatures. This means that petrol gradually thickens and hardens as it gets colder. If the consistency of a fuel is altered it naturally affects the performance of the engine it is powering. This is a major safety issue with aeroplanes as the external temperature of a high-flying jet can be −80°F. The last thing you want to happen to a plane is for the fuel pipe to freeze up! This is where anti-freeze agents come into play; their job is to maintain the viscosity of the fuel, i.e. its ability to resist changes in the arrangement of its molecules (the kind of thing that happens when a liquid freezes).

Q —

Why is the moon sometimes visible during the day?

A —

The moon is 33,000 times brighter than Sirius (The Dog Star). That is why you can still see it during the day. The moon is visible during the day on almost every day of the lunar month except when there is a new moon or a full moon. A full moon is invisible during the day because then it is opposite the sun with the

Earth in between. It's shining brilliantly on the other side – the night side – of the Earth.

Q –

What's the difference between eau de toilette and aftershave?

A –

It's all about three things – the amount of essential fragrance oil used, staying power, and where you apply each product. Eau de toilette (usually called 'cologne' in the USA) has between 4% and 8% fragrance oil content, aftershave has only 1% to 3%. Because of the higher oil content eau de toilette tends to last much longer and, depending on skin chemistry, can last almost all day. Aftershave, on the other hand, will tend to fade after an hour or two. Finally, where to apply! Eau de toilette should be applied to pulse points on the wrists, neck or chest, where the warmth of the blood passing close to the skin's surface helps to diffuse the perfume. It should never be applied to the face as the higher concentration of essential oil will cause irritation. Aftershave is specifically designed to be applied to the face and, although it might sting like hell, it won't do your skin any harm!

Q —

How can a plane still fly when it is upside-down?

A —

At all times when an aircraft is flying its wings must be tilted so that, as they cut through the air, they force air downwards. The wings can only fight against gravity if they are pushing air downwards. When a plane is flying upside-down the pilot simply uses the control surfaces ('flaps') to tilt the plane so that the wings are still forcing air downwards.

Q —

Is it possible to loop or roll a jumbo jet?

A —

Nobody has been foolish enough to try! Apparently a Boeing test pilot did barrel roll a 707 in a reckless moment and the general consensus is that a 747 (a jumbo) could do the same, but it is an expensive piece of kit to be playing with. As to a loop, there is doubt as to whether a 747 could achieve enough forward speed to achieve the extra lift that a loop requires. Don't try it at home anyway!

Q —

Who invented the motorbike?

A —

Gottlieb Daimler built the first motorcycle in 1885.

Q —

Why does the needle on my weighing scales not stay steady when I stand on it?

A —

If, while standing on sensitive scales, you take your pulse at the wrist, you will observe that the small upwards movement of the scale's needle coincides with the beat of your heart.

The answer lies in classical Newtonian mechanics: every force causes an equal and opposite force. The object exerting the force is the blood being ejected down the descending aorta. The scales record the thrust of this rapid ejection of a mass of blood, which makes the needle wobble.

Q —

I don't remember much about Irish inventors and scientists from school. What are our national claims to fame?

A —

They really are too numerous to mention! But here are ten of the best. Maybe you will be encouraged to find out more about your scientific heritage!

1 Sir Francis Beaufort (1774–1857)

In 1805 Navan man, Sir Francis Beaufort, conceived the wind force scale which bears his name. He was a distinguished naval commander and his 13-point 'Beaufort Scale' was adopted by the British navy in 1838.

2 Robert Boyle (1627–1691)

Robert Boyle made many key contributions to the scientific revolution of the 1600s. His most famous discovery of pressure-volume relationship in laboratory conditions now bears his name; Boyle's Law (that gas pressure and volume are inversely proportional at constant temperature) was to prove fundamental to our understanding of gases and atmospheric pressure.

3 Rev. Nicholas Callan (1799–1864)

Born in Dromiskin, County Louth, Rev. Callan invented the induction coil (1836) and the self exacting dynamo (1838), both of which are still being used today.

4 Aeneas Coffey (1780–1852)

Dublin man Aeneas Coffey invented the world's first heat-exchange device in 1830. Coffey's patent still was a very efficient apparatus that led to many advances in whiskey distilling.

5 Harry Ferguson (1884–1960)

Nicknamed the 'mad mechanic', Harry Ferguson designed and built a new plough which was coupled to the tractor in three-point linkage, so forming a single unit. The Ferguson System, patented in 1926, was to revolutionise farming. Ferguson also designed and built his own motor cycle, racing car and plane - becoming the first Irishman to fly in 1909.

6 Arthur Leared (1882–1879)

Leared was a Wexford doctor who invented the modern binaural (double earpiece) stethoscope in 1851. He also discovered the importance of pancreatic juices in the digestion of fats.

7 Sir Charles Parsons (1854–1931)

Charles Parsons was from Birr, County Offaly. He invented the world's first steam turbine using vaporised water to power a rotor directly, as opposed to driving pistons. Parsons' innovation encouraged further developments in powering ships and in generating electricity.

8 Francis Rynd (1811–1861)

In 1844 Francis Rynd, a Dublin-based doctor, invented the hypodermic syringe and administered the world's first subcutaneous injection at the Meath hospital.

9) *John Tyndall (1820–1893)*

A native of Leighlinbridge, County Carlow, John Tyndall was the founding father of nephelometry (you may well ask – it's all about the 'thickness' of liquids) and was one of the first scientists to recognise the Greenhouse Effect. His invention of the 'light pipe' also laid the foundation for developments in fibre optics. (*See* 'Why is the sky blue?' next)

10) *Ernest Walton (1903–1995)*

Ernest Walton was a native of Dungarvan, County Waterford. In 1932, Walton and John Cockcroft became the first people in history to artificially split the atom, beginning the nuclear age. Walton and Cockcroft had proved Einstein's famous equation ($E=mc^2$) and successfully converted matter into energy. In 1951 they were jointly awarded the Nobel Prize for Physics, making Walton Ireland's first and only Nobel science laureate.

Q —

Why is the sky blue?

A —

The white light from the sun is a mixture of all the colours of the rainbow (the spectrum). The colours of light are distinguished by their different wavelengths. On a clear, cloudless day the sky is blue because molecules in the air scatter shorter wavelength blue light from the sun more than they scatter red light. (At dawn and dusk it is the longer wavelength red light which we see.) The first person to explain why the sky appears to be blue was Irishman John Tyndall, in 1859.

Q —

Is it true that pure water is not a conductor of electricity?

A —

Yes, pure water is in fact an insulator, meaning it does not conduct electricity well. But, because water is a great solvent, it usually has other substances dissolved in it. Any such impurities in the water will cause it to become a conductor of electricity.

Q —

If salt melts ice on roads, how do icebergs stay solid?

A —

Road salt works because the freezing temperature of a water and salt mixture is lower than the freezing temperature of plain water. If the air temperature is warmer than the freezing temperature of the ice/salt mix the ice will melt, but the precise freezing temperature depends on the amount of salt.

You have to use quite a lot of salt to have an effect on frozen roads, enough to lower the freezing point to -10°C (15°f) or less. However, the ocean is much less salty, only about 3.5 %, and freezes at -3°C (27°F). As long as the temperature stays below this point, icebergs won't melt. In the Arctic and Antarctic temperatures are below this level for most of the year.

However, icebergs do melt eventually. As they are carried into warmer waters by ocean currents they melt faster and faster but they are so big that it can take them years to melt away completely.

Q —

My daughter spilt milk in my car. It is a pretty large quantity and has hardened in the carpet. It smells like something died! Can you help?

A —

The dreadful smell is caused by decomposition of an organic material (milk). You have to stop the decomposition process and for that you need enzyme digesters, as found in biological washing powders. If you have a carpet cleaner at home you can wash the car's carpet with a biological powder and use the carpet cleaner to remove most of the moisture. Alternatively, you could get the car valeted and let some other poor devil have the pleasure!

Q —

Is there a right way to hang a toilet roll?

A —

Apparently it tears more easily if you leave the paper hanging from the back.

Q —

How does a lie-detector work and how can I get my girlfriend to take a test?

A —

The lie-detector, or polygraph, measures a number of different signals from the subject's body. When somebody takes a polygraph test four to six sensors are attached to them. These measure breath rate, pulse rate, blood pressure, perspiration, and sometimes arm and leg movement. At the start of the test the examiner will ask a few simple questions to establish a normal rate for the subject's signals, which are recorded on a single strip of moving paper. When the real questions start any change in the subject's signals will be recorded and the polygraph examiner can observe these both during and after the test. In general, any significant change in vital signs, e.g. faster heart rate or higher blood pressure, will be an indication that the subject is lying.

Regarding part two of your question, asking your girlfriend to take a polygraph test would not normally be considered a foundation for a meaningful relationship.

Q —

What does 'wifi' stand for and can you get it in Ireland?

A —

Wifi is short for 'wireless fidelity' and is a wireless system for your laptop or pc. It removes the need for wires when connecting to a wifi network, for example at work. You can also go online 'wireless' if you are in what's known as a wifi hotspot, e.g. a hotel which is wifi enabled. There are a few wifi hotspots around Ireland. A quick search on the Internet will reward you with an up-to-date list.

Q —

How does Sudocrem work?

A —

Most well-known as a treatment for nappy rash in babies, Sudocrem works in two ways. It is made up in a base with water-repellent properties which forms a protective barrier, stopping any irritants (urine, etc) from coming into contact with the skin. It also has emollient constituents which can help to soothe sore and inflamed skin.

Q —

What is the liquid contained in a spirit level?

A —

The spirit level is an ingeniously simply device for determining whether a surface is perfectly horizontal. It was invented in France in the seventeenth century. It consists of a slightly bent transparent tube held in a wooden or metal frame. The tube contains a small amount of alcohol, ether or similar fluid but is not filled to capacity so it also contains a small bubble. The position of the bubble within the tube indicates whether the instrument is perfectly horizontal.

Q —

Is there a name for the yoke a doctor uses to measure your blood pressure?

A —

Yes, it is called a sphygmomanometer.

Q —

I was wondering why are the windows in ships round?

A —

Portholes are round for the same reason that aircraft windows are round. The vehicle is subject to flexing and mechanical stress. If the windows had corners these stresses would concentrate there and eventually lead to material fatigue and cracking. With round windows the stress is evenly distributed. Very large ships, such as cruise liners, do sometimes have rectangular windows but this is only possible because the local stresses are smaller.

Q —

What exactly is a CAT scan?

A —

CAT stands for Computerised Axial Tomography. The scanner combines X-rays and computer technology to show amazing detail of the inside of a person's body. It records up to 1,500,000 X-ray readings and displays them as very thin 'slices' of tissue.

Q —

Why do articulated trucks have yellow clips behind each of the wheel nuts on every wheel?

A —

The yellow clips are a safety device to warn lorry drivers if the wheel nuts are loosening. Loosening nuts is a common problem with heavy articulated lorries. The clips are fitted to the wheel nuts and all aligned in the same direction. If the driver checks them later and finds the arrows out of alignment he knows a nut is loosening and can tighten it. The clips are usually yellow to make them easy to see.

Q —

What exactly is Archimedes' Principle?

A —

Archimedes' Principle, otherwise known as the Law of Hydrostatics, states that the apparent loss in weight of a body immersed in a fluid is equal to the weight of the displaced fluid. The discovery is reputed to have been made when Archimedes stepped into his bath. So thrilled was he that he is supposed to have run naked through the streets, crying 'Eureka' ('I've found it'), much to the bemusement of his neighbours who didn't even know he'd lost it! Archimedes (287–212 BC) was a Greek mathematician and inventor who also defined the principle of the lever and is credited with the invention, among other things, of the catapult.

Q —

Who invented the mobile phone?

A —

It not so much that it was invented as developed over a period of time. Edwin H. Armstrong invented mobile frequency modulation (FM) radio in 1935 and the first radio telephones came into use in America in 1946. However, because the number of radio frequencies in a given area is very limited, the number of possible phone calls was also limited. To solve this problem cell technology was developed so that a number of small areas (cells) could share the same frequencies. As a caller moved from one area to another the call would switch automatically. This concept was devised by a team of researchers at Bell Laboratories in 1947 but the computers of the day were not powerful enough to handle the switching. Cell phone technology developed along with improvements in computer technology and continues to do so.

Q –

Is it true that a coin dropped from the Empire State Building could seriously hurt someone on the ground?

A –

This is a frequently asked question, although sometimes the building in question is the Eiffel Tower. The maximum speed a coin dropped from approximately 1,000 ft could reach is 175 mph and you would certainly know about it if it hit you. However, this speed assumes no air currents or updrafts which would slow the coin down. It is also likely that coins dropped from high buildings will never reach the ground but will hit the side of the building and be caught in a protrusion or setback. In spite of all this, and for the safety of pedestrians everywhere, please keep your small change in your pockets!

Q —

How did Epsom Salts get their name?

A —

In 1618 a farmer in Epsom, England, tried to get his cows to drink local well water. They refused to take the water and it was found to have a bitter taste. However, although undrinkable, the water was observed to have the power to assist healing of scratches and rashes. The fame of 'Epsom Salts' spread and they were eventually recognised as magnesium sulphate.

Q —

How do hovertrains work?

A —

You are probably thinking of Maglev trains, which are suspended above a guide rail by powerful magnets. The attraction and repulsion of magnets on the train and on the tracks allow the train to travel friction-free at speeds of up to 300mph.

Q —

What's the liquid that can sometimes be seen dripping from a car's exhaust pipe when the engine is running?

A —

It's nothing to worry about. It is simple condensation, formed when hot air from the engine reaches a cold exhaust pipe.

How much does Alex Ferguson spend each year on chewing gum?

Q —

Where did the Golden Goal originate?

A —

The Golden Goal was introduced by the English F.A. on an experimental basis during the 1994-95 Autoglass Windscreens Shield. The rule was designed to do away with the dreaded penalty shoot-out. If the score was level at full-time, the teams would play two periods of 15 minutes. If either team scored at any point in either period, they would be declared the winners of the match.

The first Golden Goal was scored by Iain Dunn of Huddersfield in the 107th minute. He was presented with a Golden Football Trophy to mark this occasion in footballing history. The first golden goal to decide a major tournament came in the Euro '96 Final at Wembley when Oliver Bierhoff scored in the 95th minute to give Germany a 2-1 victory over the Czech Republic. The first World Cup Golden Goal was scored in France in 1998. Lauren Blanc's goal in the 114th minute earned France victory over Paraguay.

Because the Golden Goal rule was not universally popular it was downgraded to a 'Silver Goal'. Now if a team scores in the first period of extra time, the game continues to the end of that period before they are declared winners. If the teams are level after the first period of extra time, the second period is played in full. If the score is still deadlocked after extra time, the match is decided by, guess what, the dreaded penalty shoot-out!

Q —

Why are medicine balls so called?

A —

From grapefruit to basketball size, and weighing anything from two to thirty pounds, the medicine ball has been around since the First World War. Legend has it that medicine balls were first used on transatlantic ships; navy medics stuffed kapok (silky fibres) and rags into leather basketballs to give the seasick or bored crew some meaningful exercise.

Q —

Which is the most popular team sport in Ireland?

A —

Gaelic football is the most popular team sport with approximately 250,000 participants. Soccer is the second largest team sport, followed by hurling.

Q —

In rugby, what is the Triple Crown?

A —

The Triple Crown is awarded to one of the Home Nations (England, Ireland, Scotland, Wales) if they succeed in beating the other three during the annual Six Nations Championship. The other two countries competing in the Six Nations are France and Italy. If one team manages to win all of its matches it wins the Grand Slam. If a Home Nation wins the Grand Slam it will also have won the Triple Crown.

Q —

In poker, what is a 'dead man's hand' and how did it get its name?

A —

The hand was named after the cards held by US Marshall Wild Bill Hickok when he was shot to death – black aces, black eights and the nine of diamonds. Today the dead man's hand contains a pair of aces and a pair of eights.

Q —

What is the oldest golf course in Ireland?

A —

The Royal Belfast opened in 1881 and was followed by the Curragh Golf Club in 1883.

Q —

When were the first Olympic Games held?

A —

The first recorded Olympic Games were held at Olympia in Greece in 776BC. They were held every four years thereafter until AD393. After a lapse of some 1,500 years the games were revived in 1896 – these first games of the modern Olympic era were held in Athens.

Q —

Why don't winning Formula One drivers get laurel wreaths any more?

A —

The tradition of awarding a wreath of laurel leaves to a victor goes back to ancient Greece and Rome. It was part of Grand Prix ritual for many years but disappeared during the 1980s. The reason? Probably the fact that it obscured too many sponsors' names!

Q —

What year did Ayrton Senna die?

A —

The former Formula One Champion was killed during the San Marino Grand Prix at Imola in May 1994.

Q —

Who holds the record for winning the most All-Ireland medals in a row?

A —

The late former Taoiseach, Jack Lynch. He won hurling medals with the Cork team in 1941, 1942, 1943, 1944 and 1946. He also won a football All-Ireland medal with Cork in 1945, making six consecutive years.

Q —

What year did the Tour de France come to Ireland?

A —

1998 – it coincided with the 200th anniversary of the 1798 rebellion.

Q —

Was Red Rum ever beaten in the Aintree Grand National?

A —

Yes, twice, by L'Escargot and Rag Trade.

Q —

Does Ronaldo have a first name?

A —

That is his first name. The Brazilian forward's full name is Ronaldo Luiz Nazario De Lima.

Q —

Why do most major golf tournaments start on a Thursday?

A —

They are usually played over four days and by starting on Thursday are timed to finish on Sunday.

Q —

What is the official height of a tennis net?

A —

The net should be 3 ft at the centre strap and 3 ft 6 ins at the posts. It is the same standard for singles and doubles courts.

Q —

At what height should a dart board be hung?

A —

The centre of the bull should be 1.73 metres vertical distance from the floor.

Q —

What is the official distance between a dart player and the board?

A —

The distance from the board to the back of the oche (the line from which you throw) should be 2.37 metres.

Q —

What club was Alan Ball with when he played for the England World Cup side in 1966?

A —

He had transferred from Blackpool to Everton for a fee of £110,000 just prior to the World Cup.

Q —

Why do Panathinaikos have a shamrock as their emblem?

A —

Well, there is no obvious Irish connection! The shamrock does grow outside of Ireland and in Greece it is known as the trifylli. It was chosen to be the Panathinaikos emblem in 1918 for reasons lost in the mists of time. They may have selected green as the team's colour because of its association with the shamrock but there was a more practical reason. Before green became the official team colour players would turn up for matches in a variety of different coloured outfits!

Q —

Who did Muhammad Ali fight in Dublin in the 1960s and was he still Cassius Clay then?

A —

It was actually 19th July 1972 when Muhammad Ali fought Alvin 'Blue' Lewis in Croke Park and won by a technical knockout in the eleventh round. He had changed his name from Cassius Clay to Muhammad Ali in 1964.

Q —

When you hit the 1, 20 and 5 in darts it is called a 'bed and breakfast' – why?

A —

The origins of this expression are linked to the price of a one-night stay in a typical English bed and breakfast. It refers to a common three-dart score of 26 – made up of 20, 5 and 1. The cost of a B & B at the time of the phrase's introduction into darts slang was either two and six (two old shillings and sixpence) or two pounds and sixpence, depending on which source you believe. Hence, 2 and 6 (26).

How many GAA clubs are there in Ireland and which county has the most clubs?

There are a total of 2,857 clubs currently affiliated to the GAA, of which 312 are outside Ireland. These 312 are distributed thus:

Australia	–	70
Britain	–	88
Canada	–	13
Europe	–	21
New York	–	50
North America	–	70

That leaves a total of 2,545 clubs in the 32 counties, divided between the provinces in the following way:

Connaught	–	223
Leinster	–	1,075
Munster	–	664
Ulster	–	583

The counties with the greatest number of clubs
are:

Cork	–	259
Dublin	–	211
Wexford	–	187
Meath	–	153
Antrim	–	108

Was there ever a time when drivers kept gloves in their glove compartments?

If Neil Armstrong was the first man on the moon, who was holding the camera?

Q —

In *Sesame Street* was Bert orange or yellow?

A —

Bert was yellow and Ernie was orange. You can remember with the help of a little alliteration – Bert the banana and Ernie the orange! And yes, these things are important.

Q —

Who was the cartoon character with the catchphrase 'Heavens to murgatroyd'?

A —

Snagglepuss is the guy you are looking for. He first appeared in the *Yogi Bear Show* in 1961 but subsequently had 32 episodes all to himself. His other famous catchphrase was 'Exit stage left'.

Q —

Were there any female Smurfs?

A —

Actually, there were three female Smurfs. Smurfette was the first. She was created by Gargamel to destroy the Smurfs but Papa Smurf's magic changed her nature. Smurfette loved flowers and the colour pink. Sassette Smurfling was created by the Smurflings as a sister for themselves and Smurfette. Sassette was a sporty kind of girl with red hair and freckles. She wore pink overalls. Nanny Smurf was, guess what, a nanny to the Smurfs! She had a pet named Smoogle.

Q —

What was the name of the strong Smurf with the tattoo?

A —

His name was Hefty. He was distinguished by a

heart-shaped tattoo on his arm. He was the strongest Smurf and could always be depended upon if there was hard work to be done. He could also be a bit of a lout but everyone loved him!

Q —

What was the theme tune to *Monty Python's Flying Circus*?

A —

It was a march, composed by John Philip Sousa, called Liberty Bell.

Q —

Did Oscar from *Sesame Street* have a pink elephant?

A —

Yes, he did. Its name was Fluffy.

Q —

What are the origins of the game Rock, Paper, Scissors?

A —

This is the game in which two players each make a fist and then chant 'rock, paper, scissors' (or 'one, two, three, go') while bouncing their fists. On the last syllable the fists are opened to resemble one of the three 'weapons':

Rock   - clenched fist
Paper   - all fingers extended,
             palm sideways, thumb up
Scissors   - palm sideways, forefinger
             and middle finger
             forming 'V' shape.

The object is to defeat your opponent by selecting a weapon which defeats their choice: rock blunts scissors, scissors cut paper, paper covers rock.

The game originated in Egypt around 2,000 B.C. and found its way into ancient Greece and Rome. In Rome it was called *micatio* and later *mora*. It was so popular in fact that the Romans referred to it in a proverb to denote a trustworthy person – *dignus est quicum in tenebris mices*, which meant 'so honest that you could play mora with him in the dark'. This game was even used to settle minor disputes.

Q —

Does anyone else remember a cartoon called *The Snorks*?

A —

No, but that doesn't make them a figment of your imagination. The Snorks were a short-lived creation of Hanna-Barbera, based on characters from a Belgian comic. They lived underwater and had breathing tubes protruding from their heads. Sounds like the stuff of nightmares!

Q —

Who was the interviewer who was hit by Grace Jones?

A —

The late Russell Harty was hit about the head several times when Ms Jones felt he wasn't giving her his full attention!

Q —

What was the name of the spaceship in the cartoon *Battle of the Planets*?

A —

It was the *Phoenix*, transmuting in times of emergency to the *Fiery Phoenix*.

Q —

What was the name of Buck Rogers' little robot?

A —

The wisecracking robot was called Twiki.

Q —

When did *Dallas* start and end and did the devil appear in the last episode?

A —

Dallas was first broadcast in 1978 and ran until 1991. In the final, fantasy episode the devil did appear, played by Joel Grey.

Q —

What did J R's initials stand for?

A —

He was John Ross Ewing.

Q —

In the television series *The Professionals* what were the Christian names of the two main characters?

A —

Martin Shaw played Raymond Doyle and Lewis Collins was William Andrew Philip Bodie.

Q —

In *James and the Giant Peach* what were the names of James' two aunts?

A —

In the Roald Dahl book the orphaned James is sent to live with his wicked Aunt Sponge and Aunt Spiker.

Q —

What was the name of the fort in the old TV series *F Troop*?

A —

Running during the mid-sixties, *F Troop* featured the antics of a group of post–American Civil War soldiers stationed at Fort Courage.

Q —

What is the name of Dennis the Menace's dog?

A —

Gnasher!

Q —

What was the name of the village used in the filming of *The Prisoner*?

A —

It was the Welsh village of Portmeirion, designed by Clough Williams-Ellis.

TRADITION

Why is it that the older men get, the higher up their waists they fasten their pants?

Why, when you meet an off-road vehicle on a narrow road, do they never actually go off road but force everyone else to?

Q —

What are the names of Santa's reindeer?

A —

Santa originally had eight reindeer called: Dasher, Dancer, Prancer, Vixen, Comet, Cupid, Donner and Blitzen. He acquired Rudolph the Red Nose with the writing of the popular Christmas song!

Q —

Why do we leave out stockings for Santa?

A —

According to tradition, Saint Nicholas (Santa) left his very first gifts of gold coins in the stockings of three poor girls who needed wedding dowries. The girls had hung their stockings to dry by the fire.

Q —

During Prohibition why were drinking dens called 'speakeasies'?

A —

The term dates from the late nineteenth century and applies to any place where alcohol is sold and drunk illegally. It was common slang during the Prohibition years in the US and refers to the practice of speaking softly so as not to attract unwelcome attention.

Q —

How did six feet become the standard depth for burying people?

A —

It was in London during the Great Plague of 1665 that a depth of six feet became a legal requirement for burials. Nobody knew how this killer disease was transmitted (it was of course by fleas from rats) and it was thought that burying corpses more deeply might stop the plague from spreading.

While '6 feet under' remains common slang for 'dead and buried', many burials are now at a much shallower depth. Some UK county by-laws only require that a coffin be covered with a minimum 30 inches of soil. In the USA it can be much less; in California, for example, coffins must be covered by at least 18 inches of dirt and turf. Somehow 'one-and-a-half feet under' doesn't sound as if it would make a good title for a TV show!

Q —

Is it true that St Valentine is buried in Dublin?

A —

It is impossible to separate fact from legend in the case of St Valentine (or Valentines – there are at least three saints of the same name!) but the remains of the patron saint of lovers are reputed to reside in the Carmelite church in Whitefriar Street, Dublin. The body of the saint was apparently a gift to Father John Spratt from

Pope Gregory XVI. The story goes that Fr Spratt visited Rome in 1835 and the Pope was so impressed by his preaching that he gave the good friar a gift of the saintly remains. St Valentine was duly disinterred from the Cemetery of St Hippolitus in Rome and brought to Whitefriar Street in 1836.

Q —

Who invented traffic lights and why did they pick red and green?

A —

The first traffic lights were manually operated gas lanterns installed in London around 1868. The signal used two colours – red for 'stop' and green for 'caution'. One day a lantern exploded and injured the policeman who was operating it. Obviously a more efficient traffic signalling system was needed! The railways were already using a red/amber/green signalling system and in 1920 an enterprising policeman, William Potts, from Detroit, Michigan, decided to try the same system for road traffic. Around the same time, the prolific African American inventor, Garrett Morgan, patented the precursor to the automatic traffic lights still used today.

The choice of the colours red and green was probably based on the standard human emotional response to each. Red is almost universally seen as a danger signal – we talk of 'seeing red' when we are angry – and would be a natural warning colour. Green, on the other hand, evokes very different emotions and is usually calming. It is seen as the colour of nature and abundance. Yellow or amber are less easy to fathom as they are associated with warmth, happiness, and the sun – lazy rather than cautious connotations. However, it is a colour which contrasts well with green and red, is highly visible but not too harsh on the eyes of motorists.

Q —

Why are Dubliners called Jackeens?

A —

Jackeen is a diminutive of Union Jack, coined by country people who saw Dubliners as supporters of British rule in Ireland.

Q —

What is the name of the leaf that is supposed to neutralise a nettle sting?

A —

The most commonly used antidote to stinging nettles is the dock leaf. Interestingly the dock plant is often found growing conveniently close to wild nettles. If you have no dock handy, mint, sage or rosemary leaves rubbed on the skin will also give some relief.

Q —

Why do Australians wear corks on their hats?

A —

This type of headgear was invented by Australian Aborigines. The wide brim protects from the sun and the dangling corks keep flies off the wearer's face.

Q —

I recently went to see *Playboy of the Western World* – can't for the life of me remember why they refer to the police as 'Peelers'.

A —

For the same reason that the British police are often referred to as 'Bobbies' – both are named after the founder of the two forces, Sir Robert Peel. He established the Royal Irish Constabulary in 1812. This police force was so successful that he decided to emulate it in London. In 1829 the Metropolitan Police Act was passed, providing for a permanent, paid police force.

Q —

What have nuts to do with Halloween?

A —

Nothing specifically, but seasonal fruits, vegetables or flowers tend to become associated with traditional festivals or events. Nuts are ripe at Halloween and so have become associated with that festival and also with Christmas. Likewise, we think of the lowly Brussels sprout as a Christmas vegetable and it is traditional to eat strawberries at Wimbledon!

Q —

Why are all plane doors on the left-hand side?

A —

Well observed! We checked with Aer Lingus, who informed us that planes do have doors on both sides but it is an industry standard that the left-hand side is used for passengers embarking and disembarking. In addition, all airports are designed with passenger ramps to meet the left-hand side of incoming planes. The door on the right-hand side is used by maintenance crews.

Q —

Why do soldiers salute?

A —

The origins of the salute are uncertain but the most popular theory is that it began in late Roman times when assassinations were common. A citizen wishing to see a public official was obliged to approach with his right hand raised to show that he was not holding a weapon. (What if he was left-handed and ill-intentioned?) In the Middle Ages knights in armour raised their visors with the right hand to greet a comrade and the practice gradually became a way of showing respect. In the early to mid-twentieth century, when men commonly wore hats, it was considered courteous to remove it with the right hand on greeting a lady. The military salute is a distillation of these traditions and is a formal greeting and mark of respect.

Q —

Why is the toucan associated with Guinness?

A —

The toucan first appeared as a Guinness character in 1935, although he was meant to be a pelican! The famous Guinness artist, John Gilroy, had devised a 'Guinness a day' promotion which used a pelican with seven pints on its beak. Unfortunately, the copy was considered mildly offensive; it read:

A wonderful bird is the pelican,

Its bill can hold more than its belly can.

It can hold in its beak

Enough for a week,

I simply don't know how the hell he can.

The novelist Dorothy L. Sayers, creator of *Black Beauty*, was then working as a copy writer and was asked to come up with an alternative rhyme. Her version was:

If he can say as you can

Guinness is good for you,

How grand to be a Toucan,

Just think what Toucan do.

Thus the pelican became the toucan and was associated with Guinness for the next fifty years.

Q —

Why do all Eircom drivers have their lights on during daylight hours?

A —

About twelve years ago Eircom instigated a safety programme for their vehicles called 'Be Safe, Be Seen'. All Eircom vehicles at the time had their lights automated so that they would come on with the ignition. Some of their newer vans are not automated but all drivers are instructed to have their lights on at all times. Have you noticed that all Volvos have their lights on too? They have automatic parking lights. In some countries, like Sweden, it is illegal to drive without your lights on. So now you can stop flashing your own lights at Eircom drivers, Volvo owners and people from Sweden!

Q —

What's the significance of holly at Christmas?

A —

As with many Christmas traditions the gathering of holly dates back to pagan times. In pre-Christian days particular significance was attached to anything which retained the appearance of life when all around nature was dying. Holly and mistletoe were both impressive to our ancestors because they stayed green and bore berries during the winter months. The holly was incorporated into Christmas celebrations because its spikes were thought to represent Christ's crown of thorns and the red berries His blood.

Q —

Who invented Christmas crackers?

A —

Tom Smith, who was a baker of wedding cakes, from Clerkenwell in London. On a visit to Paris in 1840 he came across bon-bons, sugared almonds wrapped in a twist of paper. He brought the new sweets back to Clerkenwell, where they were a great success. He began putting sentimental mottoes on slips of paper inside when he noticed that young men were buying them for their sweethearts. A few years later he was standing beside a fireplace when a crackling log gave him the idea of adding sound effects to his sweets. After much experimentation, and bearing the scars to prove it, he perfected the first cracker in 1846.

Q —

What is the correct order of speeches at a wedding?

A —

The traditional order of speeches is: father of the bride, the groom, the best man. If the bride wishes to make a speech this should come immediately after the groom's.

Q —

Why do we wear wedding rings on the third finger of the left hand?

A —

Before the details of the circulatory system were fully understood it was generally believed that a vein ran directly from the third finger of the left hand to the heart. The heart being seen as the seat of all emotions, it was considered appropriate for wedding rings to be worn on the third finger of the left hand, acknowledging the hand/heart connection and symbolically declaring love for your spouse.

Q —

Where did the idea of godparents come from?

A —

The tradition of godparents goes back to early Christian times. When pagans wanted to convert to Christianity they would offer themselves for baptism by the local bishop. He would ask them to find a Christian friend who would vouch for their genuine desire to convert and would promise to support the convert in becoming a faithful member of the church. Such friends were the first godparents.

OUR PLANET

If the world is really round why do spirit levels show it to be flat?

If the tide is in on the west coast of Ireland is it out on the east coast of America?

Q —

What's the story with the Taj Mahal (and I don't mean your favourite take-away!)?

A —

Then you must mean the mausoleum of Mumtaz Mahal at Agra in India. This is held by many to be one of the most beautiful buildings in the world. Constructed entirely in white marble, inlaid both inside and outside with precious gems, the Taj took 22 years to build. It was completed in 1648 and is considered a masterpiece of Islamic architecture. Its construction was ordered by the grieving Mogul Emperor Shah Jahan as a memorial to his wife, Mumtaz Mahal, whose grave is housed in the lower chamber. The Taj Mahal is one of the world's greatest tourist attractions and is reputed to be most stunning when viewed at dawn or sunset.

Q —

What are the Northern Lights?

The Aurora Borealis, the bright dancing lights seen in the far northern skies, are collisions between electrically charged particles from the sun with gaseous particles in the Earth's atmosphere. The temperature above the surface of the sun is millions of degrees Celsius. At this temperature, collisions between gas molecules are frequent and explosive. Free electrons and protons are thrown from the sun's atmosphere by the rotation of the sun and escape through holes in its magnetic field. Blown towards the Earth by the solar wind, the charged particles are largely deflected by the Earth's magnetic field. However, the Earth's magnetic field is weaker at either pole and therefore some particles enter the Earth's atmosphere and collide with gas particles. The lights are also seen above the magnetic pole in the southern hemisphere and are known as the Aurora Australis.

The colours seen in an Aurora depend on the type of gas particles that are colliding. The most common colour, a pale yellowish-green, is produced by oxygen molecules located about 60 miles above the Earth. Rare, all-red auroras are produced by high-altitude oxygen, at heights of up to 200 miles. Nitrogen produces a blue or purple/red aurora. The lights appear in many forms, from patches or scattered clouds of light to streamers, arcs or rippling curtains.

Q —

Why does the earth keep rotating?

A —

Everyday experience leads us to believe that you need energy to create momentum, i.e. that an object must be 'pushed' by a force in order to keep it moving. However, as with a lot of things, our intuition in this case is completely wrong. If an object is moving, then a force is required to slow it down or stop it, not to keep it moving. ('Objects in motion tend to stay in motion. Objects at rest tend to stay at rest'.) It is the force of friction that stops Earth-bound objects from moving forever. But for the Earth, rotating on its axis, there is no force working to counteract its rotation (except the gravitational effect of the moon, but that's working very slowly), so you don't need an energy input to keep it spinning. OK, but why is it spinning in the first place? The reason that the Earth and other solar planets move at all is that each star (like our sun) spins from the original angular momentum that was in the solar nebula from which it formed. The orbital motion and spin of the planets in our solar system are due to this original angular momentum. Now you're probably sorry you asked.

Q —

How does the moon affect the tides?

A —

The moon and the Earth exert a gravitational pull on each other; it is what keeps the moon in the Earth's orbit. The moon's gravity pulls the water of the Earth's oceans towards it and the water moves up in a slight bulge on the side of the Earth facing the moon. At the same time, however, centrifugal force is causing the water on the other side of the Earth (facing away from the moon) to be pulled out from the centre also.

The gravitational and centrifugal forces are constant, always pulling water towards and directly away from the moon, and the forces in either direction are equal to each other. The bodies of water on which these forces are exerted change constantly as the Earth rotates and thus tides are created.

Q —

Is it the clock or the bell that is called Big Ben?

A —

The clock tower on the British Houses of Parliament is called the Great Clock of Westminster. The bell, whose sound is familiar the world over, is Big Ben.

Q —

Where is Maastricht (of Treaty fame)?

A —

The Netherlands.

Q —

How many troops took part in the D-Day landings?

A —

The sixtieth anniversary of D-Day was celebrated on 6th June 2004. On 6th June 1944, 156,000 troops were landed on the Normandy beaches, including Britons, Canadians and Americans. By the end of 11th June (D-Day + 5) 326,547 troops and 54,186 vehicles had been landed.

Q —

Is it true that Dublin was bombed during World War II?

A —

Yes, in May 1941 German planes bombed Dublin, mistaking it for Liverpool.

Q —

Do you have to be born in the USA to join the FBI?

A —

There are fairly stringent entry requirements for the FBI. You must be at least 23 and under 37 at the time of your appointment. You must be a US citizen or a citizen of the Northern Mariana Islands — where Ray? The Northern Mariana Islands are in the North Pacific between Hawaii and the Philippines and include the island which brings a shudder to every Irish football fan, Saipan. A political union between this former United Nations Trust Territory and the US came into force in 1975. There are numerous other entry requirements covering eyesight, hearing, general physical condition, educational qualifications, ability to drive and use firearms, and availability for assignment anywhere in the FBI's jurisdiction.

Q —

What exactly is sea level – does it not go up and down with the tide?

A —

Sea level is the standard used in calculating elevation. It is the level of the surface of the sea relative to the land, halfway between high and low tide.

Q —

Is midnight 12 am or pm?

A —

The initials 'am' stand for the Latin *ante meridiem*, which means 'before noon'. The initials 'pm' stand for *post meridiem* or 'after noon'. It is therefore technically incorrect to label either noon or midnight with 'am' or 'pm'. However, that is being pedantic and I am never that, am I? One second past midnight is officially 'am' so if you check your digital clock you should see that midnight is 12 am and noon is 12 pm.

Q —

What is the capital of Brazil?

A —

Brasilia has been the capital city since 1960. Before then it was Rio de Janeiro.

Q —

Is it true that Nottingham in England was once called Snotingham?

A —

Almost — it was actually called Snotingaham, which means 'the home of the sons of Snot'.

Q —

Is there a place in Ireland called Greencastle?

A —

We found two. One is in Donegal and is named after a thirteenth-century castle. The other is a tiny hamlet on Carlingford Lough in County Down.

Q —

Where could a body see a piece of moon rock? Is it all in America?

A —

You can usually view a piece of lunar rock in the Natural History Museum in Merrion Street in Dublin. You will find it in the meteorite display. The rock was given to the National Museum of Ireland in 1973. It is removed from display occasionally for cleaning.

Q —

How hot is the centre of the Earth?

A —

Scientists generally agree that it is around 7,000 degrees Celsius.

Q —

Where do those mad Spaniards run through the streets with the bulls?

A —

The traditional driving of the bulls to the bullring takes place in Pamplona in northern Spain. It happens during the annual Fiesta de San Fermin over a period of several days.

Q —

On American films and TV programmes they often refer to Ivy League colleges – what are they?

A —

The term Ivy League refers to eight universities and colleges in the north-eastern US, the most famous of which are Harvard and Yale.

Q —

Where were the first skyscrapers built?

A —

The first skyscrapers were built in Chicago in the 1880s.

Q —

When exactly was the Prohibition Era?

A —

Prohibition (the outlawing of the manufacture and sale of intoxicants) existed in the USA from 29th January 1920 until 5th December 1933. And you're worried about a smoking ban?

Q —

How many oceans are there?

A —

It is generally recognised that there are five oceans. These are the Arctic, Atlantic, Indian, Pacific and Southern. The latter is the most disputed as it is formed from the southern parts of the Atlantic, Indian and Pacific oceans. In reality, of course, there is only one huge ocean or sea as they are all connected.

Q —

The OECD is often mentioned on the news – what is it?

A —

It is the Organisation for Economic Co-operation and Development.

Q —

What do the letters 'ce' on toys and electrical goods mean?

A —

The CE mark is an abbreviation of '*Conformité Européene*'. By displaying this symbol a manufacturer is declaring that the product complies with the essential requirements of the relevant European health, safety and environmental legislation. The CE mark entitles a product to be legally placed on the European market and ensures that product's free movement within the single market.

Q —

Who are the Ku Klux Klan and why are they so called?

At the end of the American Civil War, in 1865, a group of southern soldiers founded the original Klan in Tennessee. They were unhappy with the outcome of the war and could not accept the emancipation of the Negro slaves. They hoped to drive the former slaves and northern settlers back to the northern states.

The Klan became more and more violent and in 1869 it was banned. After some years of inactivity it was re-established in 1915 by William Joseph Simmons and various rituals were established. The Klan reached its zenith between 1921 and 1925 when it had about five million members, mostly the very poor. Although it still exists, the Ku Klux Klan's influence was hugely diminished by the efforts of Martin Luther King and the Civil Rights Movement from the 1960s onwards.

The name Ku Klux Klan is said to come from their original title, 'Knights of Kuklos'. Kuklos is the Greek word for a circle and Klan of course means family.

Q —

I know the Berlin Wall came down in 1989 but when was it built?

A —

It was erected in August 1961.

Q —

In what year was the siege in Monasterevin?

A —

On 3rd October 1975 Dr Tiede Herrema, the Dutch managing director of the Ferenka factory in Limerick, was kidnapped only yards from his Castletroy home. The kidnappers quickly issued a demand for the release of three inmates of Portlaoise prison: Rose Dugdale, Kevin Mallon and James Hyland.

After eighteen days Dr Herrema was traced to an end-of-terrace house on an estate in Monasterevin, where he was being held in an upstairs bedroom by Eddie Gallagher and Marion Coyle. It was another eighteen days before the siege ended peacefully on the night of 7th November when Gallagher and Coyle surrendered to the police.

Gallagher subsequently served fourteen years of a twenty-year sentence and Coyle served ten years of a fifteen-year sentence. Dr Herrema wanted to stay in Ireland, despite his ordeal, but his company decided that the risk was too great.

After his return to The Netherlands the Ferenka factory closed with the loss of 1,400 jobs.

Q —

What is the point of the two cables you see bolted to the ground on your way in to some towns. Is it for monitoring speed?

A —

These are actually traffic counting tubes and are used by the National Roads Authority to monitor the number of vehicles using a particular stretch of road. They are often situated on the approach to a junction. There are usually two tubes in case one device breaks down; however, sometimes they are spaced apart in order to assess the speed of traffic. The tubes we can see are temporary and usually in place for about two to four weeks. However, some roads are fitted with permanent tubes, buried just below the surface of the tarmac for constant monitoring of traffic. The information collected is used when designing new traffic control measures for a town or busy junction.

Q —

When did the Channel Tunnel open?

A —

It opened 6th May 1994 – but wasn't it a long time coming! The idea of a Channel Tunnel was first discussed in 1802.

Q —

How many people did it take to build the Channel Tunnel?

A —

Almost 13,000 people were involved in its construction.

Q —

Can someone please tell me where Timbuktu is?

A —

Today more commonly known as Tombouctou, it is a small city in central Mali on the southern edge of the Sahara. The city was founded in the late eleventh century and became a great commercial hub and a place renowned for Islamic scholarship. Its zenith as a thriving trading and religious centre was reached in the early sixteenth century when it had a population of about 40,000. Its fortunes declined over the subsequent centuries and today its population has dwindled to an estimated 20,000.

SONGS

Why do we still talk about 'record shops' when you can buy everything but records in them?

Q —

What year did 'Rock 'n' Roll Kids' win the Eurovision?

A —

Performed by Paul Harrington and Charlie McGettigan, this was the winner in 1994.

Q —

Who sings 'the piano has been drinking'?

A —

The singer is Tom Waits. 'The Piano Has Been Drinking (Not Me)' is from the album *Small Change* and is well worth a listen.

Q —

Who sang 'Yummy, yummy, yummy, I've got love in my tummy'?

A —

'Yummy, Yummy, Yummy' was a major hit for Ohio Express in 1968. (Homer Simpson has since done his own version!)

Q —

Who sings the theme song to *Malcolm in the Middle*?

A —

The song is 'Boss of Me' by They Might Be Giants.

Q —

Who wrote 'The Fields of Athenry'?

A —

Now a popular sporting anthem, 'The Fields Of Athenry', was written in 1979 by Pete St John. The first popular recorded version was by Paddy Reilly.

Q —

Who sings the song that goes something like 'there's a bloke in the chip shop thinks he's Elvis'?

A —

That was the late, great Kirsty McColl.

Q —

What was the name of Pepsi & Shirley's hit? Nobody I know can remember!

A —

'Heartache' was a hit for the girls in 1987. It was written by George Michael. Pepsi & Shirley were backing singers for Wham!

Q —

In the John Lennon song 'Give Peace a Chance', what is bagism?

A —

At a press conference in Vienna in 1969 John Lennon and Yoko Ono climbed into a canvas bag to promote world peace. The basic idea was that we could all climb into bags and talk to each other. For some strange reason 'bagism' didn't catch on.

Q —

Is Tracy Chapman a man or a woman?

A —

D'oh! Tracy Chapman is a woman.

Q —

Did Christie Hennessy really play with Fleetwood Mac?

A —

Singer/songwriter Christie is famous for such hits as 'All The Lies That You Told Me',

'Messenger Boy' and 'Don't Forget Your Shovel', recorded by the likes of Christy Moore and Mary Black. However, in a former life he did play drums in an early line-up of Fleetwood Mac. If Mick Fleetwood hadn't come on the scene would they have been known as Hennessy Mac?

Q —

Who sings 'Suicide is Painless', the theme to M.A.S.H.?

A —

It was sung by a group called The Mash. It was written for the original movie in 1969. The music was written by Johnny Mandel and the lyrics by Mike Altman, the 14 year-old son of the film's director, Robert Altman.

Q —

Is Bon Jovi's real name Jon Bon Jovi?

A —

Sort of! His full name is Jon Francis Bongiovi Junior.

Q —

I'm looking for the theme tune to the sitcom *Cheers*.

A —

The song 'Where Everybody Knows Your Name' was written by Gary Portnoy and Judy Hart and is available on Gary Portnoy's album *Keeper*.

Q —

Who sang the Hawaiian style version of 'Over the Rainbow'?

A —

It was Israel 'Bruddah Iz' Kamakawiwo'ole, Hawaii's most popular entertainer until his death in 1997 at the age of 38. His version of 'Somewhere Over the Rainbow' is played at the end of the movies *You've Got Mail*, *Finding Forrester*, *Meet Joe Black* and *50 First Dates*. Kamakawiwo'ole was an extremely large man, weighing around 57 stone at the time of his death from respiratory failure.

Q —

In one episode of *Father Ted,* Ted sang and danced to a song called 'Shaft'. Who sings it?

A —

Isaac Hayes.

Q —

Who sings 'Young at Heart'?

A —

It was sung by the Bluebells and it reached No. 8 in June 1984. It was re-released in 1993 after being used in a Volkswagon commercial and on that occasion got to No. 1.

Q —

I heard a song recently and would like to get the full lyrics. It went 'Do not stand at my grave and cry, I am not there, I did not die'.

A —

This is actually a poem written by Mary Frye in 1932. It is frequently read at funerals. Michael Hutchence's sister read it at his graveside. There are a number of versions set to music which can be sourced on the web. The full text of the poem is:

> Do not stand at my grave and weep,
> I am not there, I do not sleep.
>
> I am a thousand winds that blow.
> I am the diamond glint on snow.
> I am the sunlight on ripened grain.
> I am the gentle autumn rain.
>
> When you wake in the morning hush,
> I am the swift, uplifting rush
> Of quiet birds in circling flight.
> I am the soft starlight at night.
> Do not stand at my grave and cry.
> I am not there, I did not die!

What is the name of the song which is playing when Richard Gere is flying Julia Roberts to the opera in *Pretty Woman*?

'Fallen', by Lauren Wood.

Q ▬

Who sang the theme tune to *Dirty Dancing*?

A ▬

Bill Medley and Jennifer Warnes. It was called '(I've Had) The Time of My Life'.

Q ▬

Who sang the song 'Hello, This is Joanie'?

A —

This was a hit for Paul Evans in 1979. Although he had written for numerous other artists his only other major hit was 'Seven Little Girls Sitting in the Back Seat' in – wait for it – 1961!

Q —

What was the name of David Gray's debut album?

A —

It was *A Century Ends*.

Q —

Remember the hit 'Pass the Dutchie' by Musical Youth? What were they singing about?

A —

This was a hit in 1982 for the young band from Birmingham. 'Pass the Dutchie' was based on a song by the Mighty Diamonds, 'Pass the

Kutchie' but, as kutchie means marijuana, it was thought best to change the lyric to dutchie, which apparently means a cooking pot!

Apart from the late George Harrison, who were the members of *The Traveling Wilburys*?

A —

They were:

Tom Petty	–	Charlie T. Junior
Bob Dylan	–	Lucky Wilbury
Roy Orbison	–	Lefty Wilbury
Jeff Lynne	–	Otis Wilbury
George Harrison	–	Nelson Wilbury

Q —

What's the story with the song 'Blinded by the Light'? Does it really say 'washed up like a douche in the middle of the night'?

A —

Again I say, d'oh! The chorus goes:

>Blinded by the light
>Revved up like Deuce
>Another runner in the night.

The song was written by Bruce Springsteen and was a huge hit for Manfred Mann's Earthband. The Deuce in question is a car.

Was Robinson Crusoe the only man ever to get work done by Friday?

Why do I only leave voice messages when I'm drunk (and then look for the 'erase' key)?

Q —

You know the way Liz Taylor and Richard Burton were married a few times, well what are the records for being married the most times?

A —

Richard and Carol Roble are the most re-married couple. They wed each other 56 times, beginning in 1969.

The most married man in history (serial monogamist) was Glynn Wolfe, a former Baptist minister from Blythe, California. He was married twenty-eight times.

The most married woman in history was Linda Lou Essex from Anderson, Indiana, who was married twenty-two times.

Q —

My wedding bill totalled €32,000. Make me feel better by telling me who has spent the most on their big day?

A —

The most expensive wedding on record was a seven-day celebration of the marriage of Mohammed, son of Sheik Rashid Ben Saeed Al Maktoum, to Princess Salama in 1981. The wedding took place in Dubai and the bill came to $44 million.

Q —

The Luas has got me wondering (even though it's a tram), how long is the world's longest railway platform?

A —

The world's longest railway platform is in India and is over half a mile long.

Q —

Who has had the most UK No.1s?

A —

At the time of their break-up in 1970 The Beatles held the record with seventeen No.1 hits. In the same year Elvis Presley scored his sixteenth with 'The Wonder of You'. It took another seven years for him to equal the record with 'Way Down', but unfortunately it was a posthumous achievement. However, The King had the last laugh; in June 2002 he topped the chart again, helped by Dutch D.J. JXL, with the remixed 'A Little Less Conversation'.

In the past 50 years only five acts have had ten or more No. 1 hits. They are Elvis Presley (18), The Beatles (17), Cliff Richard (14), Westlife (12) and Madonna (10).

Q —

Which is the world's largest religion?

A —

The top three are: 1 Christianity, 2 Islam and 3 Hinduism.

Q —

Where is the world's biggest church?

A —

It is in the Ivory Coast in West Africa. It was modelled on St Peter's in Rome and was completed in 1989. It can seat 7,000 people.

Q —

What are the statistics on Santa's workload?

A —

There are 378 million children in the world with an average of 3.5 per household. That means Santa has to visit 91.8 million homes. Accounting for different time zones across the globe, Santa has 31 hours to finish his work. This gives him approximately one thousandth of a second per visit (park the sleigh, get down the chimney, drop the gifts, eat the snack, get back up the chimney) – no wonder nobody ever sees him! To get to every child Santa's sleigh must travel at 650 miles per second (3,000 times the speed of sound) – no wonder we never hear him! Assuming the average weight of a present is 2 lbs (a box of Lego), the sleigh weighs 321,300 tons, not including Santa who carries a bit of weight himself. So how does he do it? Magic!

Q —

What is the most common surname?

A —

The most popular surname on the planet is Zhiang, the family name of approximately ten percent of all Chinese people. In the English-speaking world the most common surname is Smith.

Q —

How many possible combinations of six numbers are there in the Lotto?

A —

Apparently, 5.2 million, but we haven't tried them all yet!

Q —

Which country was the first to win the Eurovision Song Contest?

A —

You are not going to believe this but it was Switzerland!

Q —

I recently read that four out of ten American workers work in McDonald's – can this be true?

A —

According to McDonald's own statistics one in eight Americans have worked for them at some point. That equates to about $12\frac{1}{2}\%$ of the population (not 40% as your question suggests).

Q —

How many McDonald's are there in Ireland and the world?

A —

At time of going to press there are 68 McDonald's in Ireland and in excess of 31,000 in 121 countries around the world. The company also operates other restaurant brands including Aroma Café and Prêt A Manger.

Q —

How many mph does wind have to travel at to be classed as a hurricane?

A —

The Beaufort Scale (*See* Irish inventors p.129) ranges from '0', calm, to 'Force 12', hurricane. Calm means a wind up to 1 km per hour and hurricane refers to winds in excess of 118 km (65 miles) per hour.

Q —

I received a world record certificate for my birthday which said I was the youngest person in the world for 0.39 seconds at the time I was born. Is this true?

A —

It is true that a child is born approximately every 0.39 seconds so, yes, you probably did hold the world record as the youngest person on the planet momentarily.

Q —

Where is the driest place on Earth?

A —

It is the Atacama Desert in Chile, South America. In some areas there has been no rain for more than four hundred years.

Q —

How tall was/is the tallest person ever recorded?

A —

The tallest person ever recorded, for whose height the evidence is irrefutable, was Robert Pershing Wadlow. He was born 22nd February 1918 in Illinois, USA. When he was last measured, on 27th June 1940, he was just over 8ft 11in. tall. His shoe size was 37 (18½ in.) and his hands measured 12¾ in. from the wrist to the end of the middle finger (so each hand was a foot, boom-boom!). Robert Wadlow was still growing when he died on 15th July 1940.

Q —

How many men have walked on the surface of the moon?

A —

Twelve.

Q —

How deep is the deepest part of the ocean?

A —

The deepest part of the ocean is the Challenger Deep, named after the British survey ship *Challenger II* which pinpointed this area of deep water off the Marianas Islands in 1951. In 1960 the US Navy submersible *Trieste* was sent into the Marianas Trench (north-east of the Philippines) and touched the bottom at 35,813 ft (10,915 m) – that's a depth of almost seven miles and more than enough to cover Mount Everest if you could drop it into the ocean. The most recent measurements of the Challenger Deep were made by the Japanese, using a narrow multi-beam echo sounder, which indicated a depth of 35,838 ft.

The right name for the job

- There's a urologist in Limerick called Mr. Flood.

- There's a shrink in Cork called Dr. Looney.

- There's a swimming coach in Gormanstown College called Seamus Waters.

- There's a wood fabrication plant in Carrick on Shannon, specialising in doors. The owner's name is Jim Morrison.

- My grand aunt owned a pub – her name was Mrs Sherry.

- I knew a lad, he was a 400m champion, and his name was Robbie Leggit.

- One of my lecturers is Mr Chris Cross.

- The head of construction in Dublin is Mr. T Brick. It's on a sign at Dolphins Barn.

- When I was in school my music teacher's name was Mary Melody.

- There's a chemist in Ranelagh called Leech.

- There's a cabinetmaker in Dublin called Woodhead.

- I've got two mates Shane and Steven Ryder. They're twins and jockeys.

- My horticulture lecturer in UCD is called Mrs Forrest, and the head of the department is called Prof Gardener.

- There are three families in Ashbourne that live side by side called the Wrens, the Swans and the Crowes.

- I work in a chocolate factory and a colleague of mine is Gene Sweetman.

- Pete Burns works for Bord na Mona.

- I work for a software company and we had a test engineer called Luca Testa and a person in charge of documentation is called Ita Page.

- There was a teacher in the Mercy Secondary School Waterford called Miss Chawke.

- A few years ago I was with a patient who was getting a scan. The student nurse's name was Nurse Harte and the doc was Dr Kidney.

- There were three vets in Ballyhaunus, County Mayo, that shared a practice called Daly, Noon and Knightly.

- Ray I am a garda and I was stationed with a man named Sargent and he is a sergeant now.

My mum said to me last Christmas that it might be a good idea to ask people about questions children ask. Why do mums always have such good ideas? Anyway, here they are!

- Roisin, aged four, asks: 'Ray, have you ever met the little men who live in the traffic lights? Mr Green is my favourite.

- When my sister was younger she asked my dad: 'Does a cow know she's a cow?' Even to this day dad is still stumped by that question.

- When my niece Poppy was two and a half she asked her mother: 'Mammy, if my mouth didn't work would the words come out my nose?' How do you answer that? Ever since I've treated her as you would Yoda!

- My brother asked my mum after school one day: 'Were you there when Jesus was crucified?'

- My six-year-old daughter called me down to her room one night in a panic. When I got down she said: 'Oh my God, Mam, I just realised I was naked inside your belly.'

- When we buried our dead cat, our three-year-old neighbour came up with his own explanation for burial: 'Mammy, today we sowed the cat.'

- While babysitting my little cousin who was all excited trying to tell my boyfriend something, my boyfriend said: 'Come on spit it out.' The child paused for a minute and spat on my boyfriend!! So funny.

- My brother used to ask my dad all sorts of weird questions, for example: 'Can a bee sting a nettle and can a nettle sting a bee?'

- Last month during a hot spell, my four-year-old nephew was eating an ice cream and I asked him for a lick, so he came over to me and licked me on the cheek. Got what I asked for I suppose. Kids Rock!

- My little cousin asked me: 'Who hangs up the sky every morning?'

- When I was young I told my parents: ' When I grow up I want to be Chinese.'

- When my son was smaller he used to sing the first line of the national anthem – it went: 'She's a female fawn.'

- My little sister saw a person driving a car with a Labrador in the front seat and wanted to know: 'Is that his guide dog?'

- My son thought that the wheelchair parking spaces were for people to park their wheelchairs in. He was trying to work out how many wheelchairs could fit in each space. The innocence of it all!

- My son asked me: 'Was it was very dangerous when you were young with all the dinosaurs and all?'

- My brother-in-law asked while looking at a map on a car trip from Dublin to Kerry: 'Is it downhill all the way?' He was twelve years old at the time.

- When my mam was explaining the facts of life I replied: 'Yuck, you and dad did that seven times.' Little did I know!

- My little brother asked: 'What's a condom, Mammy?' Mam replied: 'It's something you put on your big toe in winter.'

- On a rare trip to Dublin as a kid, I asked my mam: 'Why are all those houses stuck together?'

USEFUL
WEBSITES

encarta.msn.com

The dictionary on this site is great for explaining the exact meaning of a word (obviously) but also offers a pronunciation via sound file and in most cases the origin of the words.

www.commercialbreaksandbeats.co.uk

Great site for finding out what music is used on ads running on TV.

www.80snostalgia.com or www.tvcream.org

Great for TV themes. There are many sites that offer theme tune downloads and there is no one site that is the be all and end all. Best tip: type the programme title and the word 'wav' into a search engine and work from there.

www.thisdayinmusic.com

It's one of the most common questions we get asked – what was number one on the day I was born? This gives you the US and UK number one on any given date as well as other little titbits.

www.howstuffworks.com

Does exactly what it says on the tin! Vast number of subjects covered and answered in great detail, often with detailed diagrams etc. Check out the page explaining how a boomerang works.

The Original Bestseller

BESTSELLER

FIXED

Answers to Ireland's
Frequently Asked Questions

Compiled from *Fix It Friday*
The Ray D'Arcy Show

'Answers the niggly questions that
baffle us' – *The Sunday Times*

'A great read' – *Sunday Mirror*

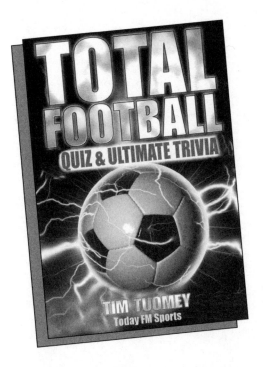

'Brilliant! A must have for every true Irish soccer fan' – *Johnny Giles*

'The Manchester United of quiz and trivia books . . . top class!' – *Gary Pallister*

'If you want to impress friends with your football knowledge, then this book is for you.' – *Kevin Sheedy*